GOD, CHRIST AND THE WORLD

£1-00 ℮

CW00953153

ARTHUR MICHAEL RAMSEY
ARCHBISHOP OF CANTERBURY

God, Christ and the World

A Study in Contemporary Theology

SCM PRESS LTD
LONDON

SBN 334 00550 1 (cloth)
SBN 334 00548 5 (paper)
First published 1969
by SCM Press Ltd
56 Bloomsbury Street London WC1

Second impression 1969
Third impression 1969

© SCM Press Ltd 1969

Printed in Great Britain by
Billing & Sons Limited
Guildford and London

CONTENTS

PREFACE

IN HIS challenging book *The Secular City*, Harvey Cox wrote that 'the real ecumenical crisis today is not between Catholics and Protestants but between traditional and experimental forms of church life'; and he added: 'If church leaders do not recognize this, within a few decades we shall see a cleavage in the church that will be comparable to the one that appeared in the sixteenth century.'[1]

This book is written in the awareness of the issues which Harvey Cox here raises. But it is concerned not primarily with the patterns of church life but with theology. I set myself in this book to examine some of the contemporary theological trends – the concepts of secular Christianity, the existentialist treatment of Christian doctrine, and some aspects of New Testament study. My conclusion is that while the historic faith of Christianity stands, and it is more than ever necessary to assert its supernatural character, it is only possible to do so convincingly if we are ready to learn much from the contemporary conflicts. In particular, if we are to convey to secularism the belief in transcendence, it must be a transcendence realized in the midst of secular life and not apart from it. So, too, the utterly

[1] *The Secular City*. New York: Macmillan; London: SCM Press, 1965, p. 160.

untenable paradox of Christianity without theism is a challenge to Christians to let their grasp of the reality of God be more truly Christocentric. Sometimes contemporary atheism means not the rejection of the God and Father of Jesus Christ but the rejection of deity as represented by many of us Christians. Sometimes, also, contemporary atheism means the refusal to accept uncritically the age-long assumption that the universe has a plan and a centre. Rather than rely upon the assumption in any facile manner it is for Christians to show that it is only in the light of the Cross that all things work together for good.

If authorship is a rash venture for one whose life of incessant busyness makes reading and writing difficult, I feel it to be right for the Church's pastors to try to grapple with the conflicts concerning belief within and without the Church and to encourage right ways of approaching them. While as a piece of writing this book is new, it represents some of the things which I have been saying in lectures and addresses to students and others in the past year and more.

I have dealt only with a selection of the theological material which might be held to be important for my theme. Thus I have omitted any direct consideration of the debate about Religionless Christianity. This is because I discussed the issues raised by Bonhoeffer in my Scott Holland lectures published in 1965 with the title *Sacred and Secular*,[2] and in an essay which I recently contributed to the volume *Spirituality for*

[2] London: Longmans; New York: Harper and Row.

Today.[3] I think it will be apparent in the present book how in the main I see worship and prayer in their relation to theology and action.

The particular selection of themes in this book is, however, suggested by the movement of its argument. Starting with the phenomenon of modern secularism I face in the first chapter the issue of transcendence as crucial for a Christianity which is authentically Christian. This leads me on to consider in the second chapter two specimens of the Death of God concepts, and the upshot of the discussion is that theism vindicates itself as a deeply Christocentric theism. So we pass on inevitably to the person of Jesus Christ, and in so doing we face at once Bultmann's challenge to traditional views of the relation of Christ to history and to doctrine. Rejecting much, but also learning much, of Bultmann, we are able to consider afresh the history of Jesus and the significance of Jesus for the understanding of God and of man. The final chapter draws together some results and considers the right way and the wrong way of recovering for our time the authority of the Bible and its message.

Since the stirring of the theological waters some five years ago by Bishop John Robinson's *Honest to God*, theology in England has to a large extent lost what we can now see to have been a long-established insularity. It was perhaps that insularity which made some of us slow to grasp what was happening. It was not that some people called 'new theologians' were

[3] London: SCM Press, 1968.

inventing theologies of compromise with the secular world: it was rather that they were trying to meet, often in clumsy and muddled ways, pressures and currents already moving powerfully in and beyond Christendom. In the present work I owe much to what I have learnt from writers in the United States. But if it is there that the radical concepts of secular Christianity have emerged, it is also there that theological work of a very constructive kind is being done, work which is able to sift the new trends and draw from them what can be turned to constructive account. My debt to the writings of Dr Arthur Vogel and Dr John Macquarrie, both of them Anglican scholars, will be specially apparent. But if these are conscious debts I do not forget that one's benefactors include those who influence one at the half-conscious level, and the authors whom I quote are only a fraction of the influences to whom I am indebted.

In recent years, as my readers will know, I have been much engrossed with ecumenical tasks and the *rapprochement* of Christian traditions, Roman Catholic, Orthodox, Anglican, Protestant. While this book has no direct bearing upon ecumenism as it is commonly understood, I dare to think it may be linked in two ways with the ecumenical task. On the one hand the integration of Christendom in the truth must include dialogue between the older and the newer standpoints within the several traditions as well as dialogue between the traditions as such. On the other hand Christians of different churches are drawn together not only by the bringing nearer of their structures and systems but by their missionary involvement in the community outside the camp. In this sense I dare to offer this little book as a tiny fragment of the prayer *ut omnes unum sint*.

The chapter on 'God Dead or Living' is based upon a lecture with that title given in the fall of 1967 at Harvard University and at Nashotah House in Wisconsin; and the chapter on 'Jesus in History' is akin to a lecture given at the International Congress on the Gospels in Oxford in September 1965 and published in Berlin in the series *Texte und Untersuchungen*.

I wish to thank Miss Barbara Lepper, my secretary, for the great help given in the typing of the whole work.

16 March 1968   MICHAEL CANTUAR:

ONE

Transcendence and the Secular City

I

CHRISTIANITY IN the West finds itself today in an uneasy relation to the new and rapid developments in contemporary culture. The changes of the last few decades have produced the phenomena known as 'the secular world' and 'the secular mind'. The word 'secular' properly means no more than 'of the age', and every generation in history is inevitably 'of the age'. But one of the marks of the new phase in our culture is the lack either of affection for past tradition or concern for a world beyond this. There is a mentality so insulated within its own secular frontiers as not to be concerned either with the past or with eternity. It is these phenomena which give to the word 'secular' its new shades of meaning.

Illustrations of the new 'secularity' come easily to mind. There is the widespread rejection of morality presented in terms of authority. There is the lack of interest in the ideas of the previous generation, and a dimming of a sense of history. There is the belief in the omnicompetence of the technological sciences to explain man and to serve his needs. There is the rejection of those otherworldly undertones which affected the outlook of earlier civilizations. And of course religious beliefs, practices and institutions are dismissed as devoid of relevance or meaning.

Such is the atmosphere which surrounds Western Christianity today. We must of course avoid exaggeration, for secularism by no means occupies the whole scene. The lines are often blurred and the frontiers are not rigid. Both in the United States and in Britain much from the older traditions still survives and shows creative power. In America there is still considerable practice of religion, as is seen in habits of church-going and in a degree of public interest in religious questions which is reminiscent of middle-class Victorian England. In England only a very few people would call themselves atheists, and while only a minority have Christian convictions which they could express and defend in a meaningful way, such pattern of ethical tradition as exists is a pattern derived from an earlier Christendom. But the ethos of secularism is strong and contagious, and the efforts of Christian evangelism often meet what can seem to be an almost impenetrable mass of secular-mindedness.

Now my purpose in this book is not to diagnose the religious scene or to deal with the problems of Christian witness and evangelism in the new situation, but to draw out some of the *theological* issues and to ask how Christian theology should respond to the environment in which it finds itself. So I begin by asking what in theological terms are the tenets of secularism.

Secularism commonly makes these assumptions which are sometimes avowed and sometimes half-consciously present:

1. The *temporal* world is the only world which exists. Eternity is irrelevant and meaningless. There can be no idea of human values which transcend realization within time and history.
2. *Religion* is to be dismissed. It involves unscientific superstitions, and can contribute no authentic knowledge about the world. It has encouraged people to resist scientific progress, and the practice of prayer and worship draws into an unreal realm of phantasy energies which should go into the world's proper business.
3. Man's *knowledge* is based solely upon observable phenomena. Thus 'positivism', though not an inherent part of secularism, is very characteristic of it.
4. Finally, the secularist believes in *the autonomous man*. Man's own potentialities of knowledge and of the effective use of it suffice for all man's needs. True, man has his frustrations, but his dignity lies in his power to overcome them, as he can and will through the right application of the sciences to his needs. Religion gives not help but hindrance as it keeps man in a state of puerile dependence and holds him back from his maturity.

It goes without saying that the secularist rejects Christianity as Western Christendom has handed it down. Inevitably the impression of Christianity is likely to be derived not from its saints and its creative thinkers but from its conventional impact, and Christianity is thus exposed to caricature, though it is a caricature for which there are plenty of historical and contemporary excuses. Christianity, some say, seems to be preoccupied with personal salvation, to be insensitive to the world around it, to be antagonistic to the development of the sciences, and to have unworthy ideas about the deity. It might be desirable to take some steps to exorcize a religion so absurd and so harmful, did it not seem that the technological age was causing its steady demise.

So Christianity and secularism confront one another. As the frontiers of churches and secular communities are seldom precisely drawn and every Christian must needs also be a citizen, the word 'confront' needs to be modified by the word 'interlock'. Secularist assumptions often interpenetrate the minds of Christian people, and, on the other hand, Christian sanctions have influence beyond the limits of committed Christian belief. But we must turn to the tasks of Christian theology.

Theology has reacted to the contemporary malaise in a number of ways. There are those whose answer is to reassert the theology of the Bible, whether in the manner of the revived near-fundamentalism or conservative-evangelicalism or in the manner of the 'Biblical theology' which, eschewing literalism and making full use of historical criticism, concentrates none the less upon the biblical categories with little attempt at interpretation to the contemporary world. Then there are those who look for a contemporary philosophical medium with which to translate the Gospel and find it in the existentialist view of man, and those who follow this way as preachers or apologists are more numerous than the specific disciples of Heidegger or Bultmann. But there are also those who follow far more radical courses and find within secularism itself new clues to the meaning of Christianity. They see secularism not wholly as the enemy but as the medium within which Christianity is to manifest itself in new ways.

It is with this new and radical phenomenon of 'secular Christianity' that we shall be concerned in this and the following chapter of this book. If there are great errors to be rejected, there are also challenging lessons to be learned.

II

I TURN now to Harvey Cox's book *The Secular City* as one which most vividly introduces the issues of 'secular Christianity'. It is in a way the least radical of the well-known books on this theme, inasmuch as its thesis is that modern secularism is not the ending of Christian belief in God, but is rather the fine flowering of God's own activity in history and the realm in which the Christian belief in God is to be revolutionized and reborn.

The Secular City has as its sub-title 'secularization and urbanization in theological perspective', and it describes the technological culture now dominant in so many modern cities as being not a contradiction of biblical truth but its genuine historical outcome. Writing as at once a biblical theologian (an ex-Barthian as one might guess) and a keen observer of contemporary social problems, Cox argues that the Lord of history has been at work in its developments from Moses and the prophets until our own time. The doctrine of creation asserted in the Bible liberates man from superstitions and enables him to apply himself to the knowledge and use of the created world, so bringing about in due time the secular and scientific culture of our contemporary world. It is the Lord's doing. Within the 'secular city' man's fulfilment is now to be found, and an outworn religious culture with its misleading metaphysics and irrelevant otherworldliness should be discarded so that man may hear God speaking in and through the human relationships and duties of secular life.

There is an eschatological note in Cox's appeal to us to move forward to God's new challenges:

This summons was always highly specific, especially with Jesus. He expected people to drop their nets, get out of bed, untie a horse, invite him to dinner. No one could doubt either that something momentous had occurred or that something quite definite was required of him.

Our preaching today is powerless because it does not confront people with the new reality which has occurred and because the summons is issued in general rather than in specific terms.[1]

God's action today, through secularization and urbanization, puts man in an unavoidable crisis. He must take responsibility in and for the city of man, or become once again a slave to dehumanizing powers.[2]

[1] *The Secular City*, p. 122.   [2] Ibid., p. 132.

In the secular city the Church is God's *avant-garde*, and Cox discusses many practical issues in the midst of what is a theological exposition, pleading for an assault upon the three tensions of 'center-city versus suburbs, haves versus have-nots, and ethnic and racial tensions'. The Church has a threefold role, *kerygma*, to proclaim that the secular city is here and is of God, *diakonia*, to reconcile and to heal, *koinonia*, to demonstrate the character of the new society: in these tasks the Church must press forward, and leave behind the irrelevancies of the past.

As exorcism was a great part of the work of Jesus, so exorcism is the Church's work today. It means the deliverance of people from the bondage of prejudices and fallacies of the present, and of the misleading religious culture of the past. This includes cultus and religious practice, which is no longer relevant, and also metaphysics, which is no longer valid, as in the secular city *functional* thinking must needs replace ontological thinking:

> Western Christendom, based partly on the biblical Gospel, partly on late Greek philosophy, and partly on pagan world-views, is over.... The synthesis of Protestantism and the bourgeois culture which came to birth in the seventeenth and eighteenth centuries and whose death spasms we have been witnessing for the past fifty years is also over. Yet in their organization, their theology, and their ways of relating to the world, our churches today are for the most part merely richer and shinier versions of their nineteenth century parents.[3]

[3] *The Secular City*, p. 220.

Cox dismisses the existentialism of Bultmann as being as powerless to speak to the secular city as is the substance-metaphysics which it rejects. The word of God for our new world must be not in metaphysical propositions or existential challenges but in summonses to action in specific matters of personal duty. We must speak of God *politically*:

In secular society politics does what metaphysics once did. It brings unity and meaning to human life and thought.[4]

We speak of God politically whenever we give occasion to our neighbour to become the responsible, adult agent, the fully post-town and post-tribal man God expects him to be today. . . . We do not speak to him of God by trying to make him religious but, on the contrary, by encouraging him to come fully of age, putting away childish things.[5]

This does not quite mean what has often been meant in the past by political preaching:

To say that speaking of God must be political means that it must engage people at particular points, not just 'in general'.[6]

What becomes of theism in the secular city? It is noteworthy that when Cox describes 'reconciliation' as one of the Church's activities the emphasis is upon reconciling men to one another and not upon reconciling them to God or to the truth. Yet God is real. There is no atheism or agnosticism in the thesis, and man has a transcendent quality:

[4] *The Secular City*, p. 254.   [5] Ibid., p. 255.   [6] Ibid., p. 256.

No doubt urban-secular man experiences the transcendent in a radically different *way* than did his tribal and town forebears. . . . It is his experience of the transcendent which makes man man.[7]

But the old language about God can mislead. Not only are its metaphysical forms unacceptable, but the 'I-thou' language is also unacceptable as it belongs to an outmoded historical sociology, and God's relation to man, 'rather than participation or confrontation', is a relation of 'alongsidedness'. God is with us, among us, in the decisions and relationships of the secular city. He is hidden. He is unknown. We can trust his purpose, but we cannot yet name him. He will show us a new name, as he showed a new name to Moses of old:

A new name will come when God is ready. A new way of conceptualizing the Other will emerge in the tension between the history which has gone before us and the events which lie ahead.[8]

Meanwhile we can face the uncertainty without fear. As the Exodus of Israel from Egypt was followed by the giving of a new name for the deity, so Christianity today is facing a transition no less bewildering in its unknown prospects but no less sure.

What are we to say to Harvey Cox's thesis? It is hard not to be moved by his insistence that the validity of Christianity must be tested by its power to grapple with life in the modern city. His sensitivity to human situations, his many practical counsels and his faith that the secular city shall be the scene of Christian

[7] *The Secular City*, p. 261.   [8] Ibid., p. 266.

obedience have given his book a wide influence in his own country. It has led many to look for a way of discipleship which is ready to leave worship, prayer and contemplation behind and to throw itself wholly into Christian action. Amid the prosperity of religious life and feeling in America, Cox's book sounds the challenge to meet God not in the beauty of Christian cultus but in a new awareness and a new action in such matters as the Negro ghettos. It recalls the words of F. D. Maurice: 'We have been dosing our people with religion when what they need is not that but the living God.'[9]

Yet the thesis is very vulnerable. Its history is arbitrary. It is hard to see the secular city as the direct descendant of the theology of the Bible, as biblical theism is but one factor amongst several, including Graeco-Roman culture, which created modern civilization and the subsequent scientific revolution. It is strange that a writer so versed in biblical studies should ignore the trend of biblical history towards not democracy but theocracy. The implications of this are nowhere discussed. But strangest of all is the uncritical admiration with which Cox regards the secular city as the climax of the divine plan in history. The admiration for technology seems derived from a latent Americanism rather than from the theological premises of the book. Is technological man as we see him today really to be taken as a kind of criterion of what man is meant to become?

[9] *Frederick Denison Maurice*, A Life, by his son, Vol. I, London: Macmillan Co., 1884, p. 369.

In short the thesis is impregnated with a kind of Pelagianism remote from its theological starting-point. Allowing that the secular city is becoming the scene in which man is to serve God – and that this service will be in a secular setting and manner with a readiness for new Christian norms – the *total* dismissal of any concern about prayer or contemplation or the deliberate seeking of God's grace is passing strange. In effect, therefore, the challenge to Christian action is vitiated by the encouragement of just that *activism* which has in the past proved to be spiritually starving. And the real issue for secular Christianity is thrown into relief. It is not the issue of religion. It is the issue of *grace*. The dividing line is not between a Christianity of religious practice and a Christianity of action. It is whether modern or secular man is self-sufficient or whether he still needs in his pride to seek those means of grace which the humble God of the Incarnation brings to him. And when man seeks the grace of God it means asking, and asking means praying, and praying means worshipping; and childlikeness and dependence are still the gateway to truth, whether man is tribal-man or village-man or town-man or city-man. With all his insights Harvey Cox is only misleading if he diverts from this: 'Woe is me, for I am lost, . . . for my eyes have seen the King, the Lord of hosts.'

III

I HAVE taken Harvey Cox's book as perhaps the most influential instance of a moderate presentation of 'secular Christianity'. He looks not for an abandonment of theism or for a rejection of transcendence, though he comes rather near to the latter. In the next chapter I shall pass on to the more radical thesis that there can be a new version of Christianity without theism. But common to all brands of secular Christianity is the impatience with transcendence as Christianity has understood it in the past.

Here Christians have not been blameless. They profess to be concerned with the world and with something else as well. And the something else has too often been pictured and presented not only as distinct from this world but also as away from it, as if man should look in one direction to serve God and in another direction to serve the world. Even when Christians have a lively interest in the world and the people in it and combine their devotion to God with compassion and humanity there can still be an apartness in their way of thinking. The apartness is enhanced when religious language is so used as to suggest that the world of religious imagery is 'other' than the world in which we live.

But, as Father Thomas Corbishley, S.J., has written, 'We can in fact get at the creator only through the world'.[10] Transcendence implies otherness and distinction, but not apartness or away-ness, and it is always *through* the world. It is through the natural that we encounter the supernatural, although the supernatural eludes the ability of the natural to exhaust its

[10] T. Corbishley, *Contemporary Christians*, London: Geoffrey Chapman, 1966, p. 35.

meaning. If it is the truth of the transcendent God, creator and redeemer, which secular Christianity so sadly misses, that truth will be presented with power and relevance by Christians who know that transcendence is always near to the world and through it.

In the modern world the concern about *persons* has had a new kind of prominence. There is a new kind of realization of the proposition, not in itself of course new, that 'people matter'. One sign of this is the vogue of existential philosophy with its insistence that truth is known not in ontological statements but in terms of personal self-realization. Another instance of this is the widespread practical concern to help people who are in distress. Another instance, of a totally different kind, is the behaviour of those who, frustrated in the desire for personal fulfilment, are almost compulsively led to try to prove themselves by achievements in sex or violence. Much indeed of the 'people matter' urge is a kind of revolt from the depersonalizing of industrial or technological existence, where the secular city fails to satisfy. And movements like the 'hippies' seem to be a revolt from an unsatisfactory established order, perhaps a sort of secular counterpart to the flight of the hermits to the desert in the fourth century. Modern man has built the secular city, and is restless within it.

Now the message of Christianity to the modern predicaments about persons is one of transcendence. Man is created by God in God's image for a life of glorifying God, a life whose present scene is this world but whose meaning reaches beyond it. It is a life of losing self in order to find it. In Christ there is seen within this world the God who is 'for man' in the totality of divine self-giving, and the man who is 'for God' in the totality of human response.

Transcendence, however, is not only a characteristic of God in his relation to the world as One other than the world as well as in the world and through the world. Transcendence is also a characteristic of man in his inherent being as man. It is through the recognition of transcendence in man that divine transcendence is more meaningfully presented. This theme has been impressively drawn out by Dr Vogel in his book *The Next Christian Epoch*.[11]

Vogel draws out the nature of the transcendence which belongs to man as man. It is an ability to be 'beyond' which is the most distinguishing feature of man's existence in the world, and it is because of our power to be 'beyond' our immediate situation that we are able to know things objectively. Thus it is true to say that transcendence is the essence of our existence as persons in the world:

Personal power is transcending power – the constant going beyond the formal, the immediate, the past and the present. Our very presence in the world gives a type of meaning to the world, but that meaning is the beginning and not the end of our lives.[12]

It is this characteristic of man's being within the world which points to fulfilment beyond the world:

[11] A. A. Vogel, *The Next Christian Epoch*, New York: Harper & Row, 1966.
[12] Ibid., p. 73.

The movement of our lives within the world indicates that we are made for something beyond the world. In our freedom we long for order; all our activities seek to impose and discover order. But the order we achieve in the world is never sufficient for our whole person, or for all persons. . . . Freedom needs a context in which to express itself . . . but it needs a context adequate to itself.[13]

The whole movement of our being seeks its completion in consummate Being . . . God is a different kind of being than we are, but we should rejoice in that fact, for if he were not different he would not be God. That is where the unrecognized anthropomorphism of the secularist's desire for conceptual clarity leads him astray; for if we won't let God be himself by being different from us we are in effect left only with ourselves – and that is where all of our trouble begins.[14]

God's difference from us constitutes his transcendence. Transcendence does not – and never did in classical thought – mean spatial separation or 'out-thereness'. Transcendence means, and always has meant, *difference*. God's transcendence opposes pantheism, not intimacy. God is always *here*.[15]

The truth of God's transcendence still stands. God is near, but God is different. God is here, but man is dependent. God's otherness is the otherness of Creator to creature, of Saviour to sinner; and it is for the creature still to worship the Creator and for the sinner still to ask for the Saviour's grace. Without this the new Christianity of the secular city will lose its identity as Christianity and will deceive itself and mislead its citizens. And, on the other hand, those who cherish God's transcendence will know that it is within the

[13] *The Next Christian Epoch*, p. 77.
[14] Ibid., p. 78.   [15] Ibid., p. 78.

secular city that it has to be vindicated and that the transcendent and the numinous are to be seen not in a separated realm of religious practice but in human lives marked by an awe-inspiring self-forgetfulness, compassion, humility and courage. Such lives bear witness that we have here no continuing city, for we are looking for a city which is to come.

TWO

God Dead or Living

THE IDEAS in Harvey Cox's *The Secular City*, for all their apparently revolutionary character, are moderate indeed compared with those to which we now turn. Whereas Cox looks for a new interpretation of theism, there are the more radical writers who present what they believe to be versions of Christianity which postulate either the demise of theism or the self-destruction of deity in history.

It is likely that these theories are already on the way out, for, in the words of S. M. Ogden:

However absurd talking about God might be, it could never be so obviously absurd as talking of Christian faith without God.[1]

But be that as it may these theories call for more study than they deserve. I cannot forget the plea of William Temple that some truth or other lurks beneath every erroneous position, and in this instance there is another plea which challenges us. Dr John Macquarrie writes:

If Christianity cannot be based on atheism one must nevertheless acknowledge that the challenge of atheism is a constant safeguard against idolatry.[2]

And idolatry can be a danger to which Christians, all unsuspecting, may be prone through idolizing dogmas

[1] S. M. Ogden, *The Reality of God*, New York: Harper & Row, 1966; London: SCM Press, 1967, p. 14.
[2] J. Macquarrie, *God and Secularity*, Philadelphia: Westminster Press; London: Lutterworth Press, 1968, p. 111.

B

and concepts, however orthodox these may be, in such a way as to blind themselves to the glory of God in the face of Jesus Christ.

I

THE FIRST of the concepts to which I turn is that of Paul van Buren in his *The Secular Meaning of the Gospel*.[3] It is a concept which may be called 'Christ without Theism'.

Van Buren bases his rejection of theism on the familiar reasoning of logical positivist philosophy. Ontological statements are linguistically meaningless, and religious language has validity not in terms of meaning 'God is . . .', but in terms of human attitudes of moral commitment and intention. But though both theism and religion are untenable in the modern scientific world Christ still has great meaning for the human race. That meaning is to be found, not in the theistic and religious norms which Jesus adopted as a man of his time and which the apostles accepted as the media in which Jesus was intelligible to them, but in the perfect embodiment in Jesus of *freedom*.

In Jesus alone in human history there is seen perfect freedom: freedom from tradition, freedom from fear, freedom from the pressures of society, freedom from self, freedom for others. It was in virtue of this freedom that Jesus wielded authority, and Easter was the moment

[3] Paul van Buren, *The Secular Meaning of the Gospel*, New York: Macmillan; London: SCM Press, 1963.

when the followers of Jesus awoke to the fact of his
freedom and were liberated so as to share in it:

Jesus of Nazareth was a free man in his own life, who
attracted followers and created enemies according to the
dynamics of personality and in a manner comparable to the
effect of other liberated persons in history upon people about
them. He died as a result of the threat that such a free man
poses for insecure and bound men. His disciples were left
no less insecure and frightened. Two days later Peter, and
then other disciples, had an experience of which Jesus was
the sense-content. They experienced a discernment situation
in which Jesus the free man whom they had known, themselves, and indeed the whole world, were seen in a quite
new way. From that moment the disciples began to possess
something of the freedom of Jesus. His freedom began to
be 'contagious'.[4]

Jesus now meant so much to them that they could not
tell the story of Jesus simply as the man who died, and
the story 'had to include the event of Easter'. By 'event'
we are apparently to understand a moment of realization
by the disciples:

In telling the story of Jesus of Nazareth, therefore, they
told it as the story of the free man who had set them free.
This was the story which they proclaimed as the Gospel for
all men.[5]

The freedom of Jesus is the real meaning of Christianity.
The theology was a transitory clothing of it. And while
theism can be no more, and there is no One to whom
we can pray, no One whom we can worship, there is a
timeless, absolute significance in the freedom of Jesus

[4] Op. cit., p. 134.   [5] Ibid., p. 134.

and we can truly speak of Christianity as the fellowship of those who know the contagion of his freedom.

The first weakness of the theory is the shakiness of its historical basis. It plainly requires a scientific historical foundation, but van Buren fits some data from the life of Jesus into his theory, with no scientific use of literary or form criticism. In fact, Jesus lived and taught in an historical context, the faith of the Old Testament, and he claimed to be the fulfilment of God's actions and promises in the history of Israel. He was the Christ. And his freedom is seen in his obedience to and in his innovations in the service of the God of the law and the prophets. This context is left out of account by van Buren. More still, the evidence of the gospels shows that the freedom of Jesus was a freedom for God and centred in God. As Dr Vogel, in his most valuable critique of van Buren's work, writes:

We have no evidence of Jesus' freedom apart from evidence that his freedom was based upon his life for God the Father. The freedom of Jesus was a God-oriented freedom. He was not just free, he was free for a reason, and that reason structured his life. Jesus was showing through his freedom that there is a source of life beyond the world, obedience to which makes one free in the world. His freedom *is* reference to a source beyond the world, to the Father.[6]

It is noteworthy that van Buren gives no exegesis of the sentence ascribed to Jesus by St Mark: 'Why do you call me good? No one is good but God alone'

[6] A. A. Vogel, *The Next Christian Epoch*, p. 37.

(Mark 10.18). If it be said that the reference to deity is only part of the contemporary theistic framework we can answer that the kind of freedom seen in Jesus is a freedom so bound up with that framework that there is no evidence for its existence apart from it.

And what of the supremacy of Jesus which is said to survive the collapse of theism? It is significant that despite the rejection of theism van Buren ascribes to Jesus a kind of 'absoluteness' still attaching to him. Jesus has, though van Buren would not put it thus, a certain quality of transcendence and a supra-historical dimension. He fits uneasily into the flat one-dimensional map of reality which is all that van Buren's positivism allows. Either the 'contagion' of Jesus – the secularist Easter – evaporates into the example of a figure who lived long ago or it possesses a more than secular-historical character. Thus what is true in the writer's thesis seems to elude the writer's own categories. While he is interested in secularism he shows no feeling for theologies which have tried to give positive meaning to the secular. And while it is Christ as an historical figure who is the pivot of his system he makes no attempt to apply historical science to his investigations of Christ.

For Christians, however, this attempt to reject theism and retain the significance of Christ has its lessons. It is all to easy for us to profess an orthodox doctrine and yet to fail to keep to the supremacy of Jesus for our own understanding of God. The heart of Christian doctrine is not only that Jesus is divine, but that God is Christlike and in him is no un-Christlikeness at all.

Our theism, Christocentric in its formulation, can sometimes fail to be Christocentric in our grasp of its meaning to ourselves and in our presentation of its meaning to others. It may sometimes be our fault when men find themselves rejecting our theism and feeling the attraction of our Christ. I shall return later in this book to the need for a more radically Christocentric grasp of the historic Christian faith.

II

WE COME now from the theory that theism is dead and Christ is supreme to the theory, which is utterly different, that God indeed existed but that he died by an act of loving self-destruction in the death of Jesus on Calvary.

The background to *The Gospel of Christian Atheism* by T. J. J. Altizer[7] is a mind steeped in the philosophy of Hegel and an imagination fired by the poetry of Blake. Unlike the rather dreary rationalism of van Buren it is a work filled with poetic and religious passion:

Can it have been of no theological significance that Blake is the most Christocentric of all poets and Hegel the only thinker who made the kenotic movement of the Incarnation the core and foundation of all his thinking?

The book is the author's answer to his own rhetorical question. It is written in a spirit of revolt akin to Blake's devotion to the crucified and Blake's antagonism to

[7] Philadelphia: The Westminster Press, 1966; London: Collins, 1967.

orthodox dogma and institutions, but its starting-point
and its centre is the event of the self-emptying of God on
Calvary.

Altizer is concerned about a 'totally incarnate Word'.
The fault of theology has been not to see that the
Incarnation means the abandonment of 'an eternal and
unchanging Word' and not to see that this involves
nothing less than the dissolution of God himself:

> The problem that the theologian refuses to confront is the
> inevitable incompatibility between the primordial Christian
> God and an incarnate or kenotic Christ. . . . Such a descent
> cannot be really meaningful unless it is understood as a
> real movement of God himself, a movement which is final
> and irrevocable, but which continues to occur wherever
> there is history and life.[8]

Deity has ceased to be deity in the transcendent sense,
and has become a dialectic process of spirit, which works
within history through men sharing in the Passion of
Jesus. As for Jesus, he is not to be thought of as the
exalted Lord, for 'the true Jesus has passed through his
death from a particular to a universal form, and
continues to be present in a forward moving and
transfiguring Word'.[9]

The concept is Hegelian through and through. It is
expressed in terms of ardent religion. 'Practical Christians', a term used often in the book, are those who
reject orthodox theism as a retrogression to pre-Calvary
doctrine and find Christ not in any religious institutions
but in those who now suffer with him in his extended

[8] *The Gospel of Christian Atheism*, p. 43.   [9] Ibid., pp. 55–56.

Passion which is the way of faith and love. The essential dogma is that God has died: 'God has negated himself by becoming flesh.'

How does the Christian know that God is dead? Because the Christian lives in the fully incarnate body of Christ, he acknowledges the totality of our experience as the consummation of the kenotic passion of the Word, and by giving himself to the Christ who is present to us he is liberated from the alien power of an emptied and darkened transcendence.[10]

It is not difficult to show the arbitrariness of the historical basis. How does Altizer's view of the Cross stand in relation to the rest of the New Testament? What are we to say of Christ's interpretation of his own death?[11] There is much misunderstanding, and even caricature, of traditional theology. Criticizing ideas of impassibility and the eternal perfection of the Godhead, Altizer says:

Even when theologians have rediscovered the *agape* or total self-giving of God, they have confined it to the movement of the Incarnation, and thus have dualistically isolated God's love from the primordial nature and existence of God himself.[12]

I do not think this gravamen can be applied to St John, St Augustine and the many Western theologians who have related the doctrine of the Blessed Trinity to the love revealed in the Incarnation and the Cross – to say

[10] *The Gospel of Christian Atheism*, pp. 111–112.
[11] Cf. pp. 86, 89–90 of the present work for the teaching of Jesus about the meaning of his own death.
[12] *The Gospel of Christian Atheism*, p. 67.

nothing of such modern exponents of orthodoxy as William Temple and O. C. Quick. Hegel seems to be a kind of Bible, and other theologies are judged not as what they are but as what they ought to be in relation to an Hegelian thesis.

The mention of St John gives the clue to the answer to Altizer's thesis. In the New Testament it is St Mark who describes the total dereliction and death of Jesus. It was darkness, destruction and apparent defeat. But St John shows that because it was self-giving love it was also glory and victory. The self-giving love of Calvary discloses not the abolition of deity but the essence of deity in its eternity and perfection. God is Christlike, and in him is no un-Christlikeness at all, and the glory of God in all eternity is that ceaseless self-giving love of which Calvary is the measure. God's impassibility means that God is not thwarted or frustrated or ever to be an object of pity, for when he suffers with his suffering creation it is the suffering of a love which through suffering can conquer and reign. Love and omnipotence are one. The teaching of St John concerning the divine glory has depths whose exploration can show us no less about God and the world than can the Hegelian mythology of Altizer.

But while the orthodox Christian can be very sure of the fallacies of the doctrine of God's self-destruction, he can do so only by a costly act of faith. It has been too common for us to talk in a rather facile way about human suffering and the suffering of Christ. We may too easily posit side by side the fact of suffering and the belief in God's ultimate sovereignty, as if to say rather naïvely: 'Men suffer, Christ suffered. That is true. But God is supreme and his kingdom will come.' In truth the sovereignty of God is no easy assertion, and the Christian dares to make it only in the light and at the cost of Calvary. Calvary is the key to an omnipotence which works only and always through sacrificial love. It is the lamb who is on the throne. Divine omnipotence and divine love (in terms of history a suffering love) are of one. And the assertion of this is meaningful when we are ourselves made one with the crucified and in his spirit can say: 'All shall be well, and all shall be well and all manner of thing shall be well.'

Let me here quote some words of David Jenkins:

The man Jesus Christ who is the embodiment of the pattern of the personalness of God is brought to nothing. He is not thereby reduced to nothing, because he is the expression of the transcendent and omnipotent God. But this transcendent omnipotence is the power of absolute love which finds true expression in going out from the pattern of personalness wholly into and wholly for the other. This is not to give love away nor to empty out what it is to be divine, but rather to give expression to what it is to be divine, to be love. Hence the bringing to nothingness is not the final reduction to nothingness but the completion of that identification which is the triumphant and free work of love whereby love works forward to fulfilment at any costs and through any odds . . . In relation to the practical problem of evil, God is neither indifferent, incompetent nor defeated. He is involved, identified and inevitably triumphant.[13]

[13] David Jenkins, *The Glory of Man*, London: SCM Press;

III

IT IS noteworthy that the exponents of secularized
Christianity are thinkers whose theological background
is that of a Barthian kind of biblical theology where there
is no interest in the sacramental view of the created
world as Catholic thought has developed it. Secularized
Christianity is often a reaction from a pietism which
sees no relation between Christianity and the world's
culture and a theology which lacks a positive doctrine
of the natural order. But it would be a mistake
to think that a sufficient answer is given to the 'death
of God' theologies by correction and assertion. The
lessons must be learnt.

One of the lessons, as we have seen, is that Christian
theism is valid only as a Christocentric theism, and more
still, it is valid only as a Cross-centred theism. It is in
the Cross that God discloses the essence of what it is
to be God. This is the true God and eternal life, says
St John, and he adds: 'Little children, keep yourselves
from idols' (I John 5.21).

Christians can be more prone to idolatry than they
realize, and their idolatries take the form of fetishism,
the devotional attachment to facts, words or concepts
which are not themselves final and are not themselves
God. Dogmatic formulations can become a fetish,
unless it is seen that they are pointers to the living God

New York: Scribners, 1967, pp. 105–106. These words are
part of a most illuminating discussion of divine omnipotence,
love and suffering.

whose reality no human language is able to express. Institutions can become a fetish unless it is seen that their glory is not their own but the glory of Christ reflected in their self-effacement. The imagery in which Christians think about God can become a fetish if it circumscribes thought about God within the circle of religious interests and ceases to convey the God who cares about everything which happens in the world. Preoccupation about God's laws can become a fetish if it allows devotion to the commands and the prohibitions to replace devotion to God whose commands and prohibitions they are. The Sacraments can become the focus of veneration instead of being windows into the sacrifice of Calvary and the actions of the living Christ. Equally the moods and phrases of evangelical piety can substitute a kind of self-contemplation for the self-forgetful contemplation of God and obedience to him. It is by a constant self-criticism of our own idolatries that we Christians can learn again and present to our contemporaries the glory of God in the face of Jesus Christ.

THREE

Beyond Bultmann

I

THE WORDS *demythologizing* and *existential theology*
will for a long time recall the influence of Rudolf
Bultmann, an influence far wider than the conscious
disciples of his theories. But the concepts are really far
older, and ever since the apostolic age a process akin
to demythologizing has been at work. And the primitive
Christian confession 'Jesus is Lord' was nothing if it
was not existential. It is in a perspective of discussion
longer and wider than the present debates that we can
best see the value, and, as I believe, the serious limitations
of Bultmann's thesis.

'Myth' is a word which alarms many Christian
believers. In popular usage it is often contrasted with
what is 'true', and the discovery that many things in
the Christian tradition which had been believed to be
'true' are relegated to the category 'myth' can be disturbing. But in the present discussion a 'myth' means
no more than a 'story' told in order to convey some
lesson, and it may be that the lesson conveyed is true
and that a story may be the only or the most effective
way of conveying it. The story of Adam and Eve in the
garden of Eden can convey powerfully the truth that
man is responsible to God and has wilfully digressed
from God's purpose for him. There, indeed, is something true. An edifying 'myth' can certainly have more

revelational value than an historical fact which carries no great significance. 'Myths', however, can vary in the degree to which they are self-explanatory in different contexts. Some will convey truth by their own inherent poetical or imaginative quality without any exposition or paraphrase, and some will lose that power and need 'demythologizing' in order that the underlying idea may be conveyed in different human situations. 'The lamb seated on the throne' could, and in some contexts still can, vividly convey 'the unity of sovereignty and sacrifice'. But a time may come when the latter phrase, a prosy proposition, needs to replace the poetic image unless some alternative poetic image is created.

Demythologizing was taking place in the apostolic age. In the teaching of Jesus there were pictures of a future coming of the Son of Man on the clouds and of the establishment of a divine kingdom described in vivid apocalyptic imagery with the details of a final judgement. In some of the sayings of Jesus these things were to happen within the lifetime of the disciples. But was it possible to expect things to happen on the scene of history just like that? Or were there underlying realities which the imagery conveyed to people in a certain setting of thought and culture in Palestine and which other imagery would have to convey to people in another setting of thought and culture? The teaching of the Fourth Gospel about the return of Christ through the indwelling of the Holy Spirit and about the realization of eternal life and divine judgement by the Christian

in the here and now, may fairly be called a 'demythologizing' of the earlier imagery. Again, the spatial
imagery of a local heaven to which Jesus was exalted at
the Ascension was seen to convey realities altogether
beyond space – the sovereignty and omnipresence of
Jesus. It would be quite untrue to say that a single
mythological frame dominated the thinking and
teaching of the apostolic age. The records contain
varieties of myth and varieties of demythologizing at
work. Factual records, myths, demythologizing propositions and sometimes – as in the Apocalypse – 're-
mythologizing' processes all had their part in the
apostolic thinking, teaching and writing about Jesus
Christ.

If, therefore, we need to be cautious in accepting a
single formula about demythologizing the New Testament, we need a like caution about adopting a single
formula concerning existential theology. From the
apostolic age onwards Christians have had recourse to a
number of philosophies in presenting to themselves
and their contemporaries the significance of Jesus
Christ. An employment of Platonism had its first begin-
nings in the apostolic age if we are right in seeing an
Alexandrine strain in the Epistle to the Hebrews. It was
a disturbing revolution when Thomas Aquinas expounded Christian belief in terms of Aristotelian
metaphysics. Dr John Macquarrie notices three kinds
of philosophy which Christian theologians have been
employing in recent years.[1] There is *process philosophy*

[1] J. Macquarrie, *God and Secularity*, pp. 92–100.

which takes for reality the world in time and space and relates the concept of deity to the understanding of nature through its many phases, with man as the climax. S. A. Alexander and A. N. Whitehead were philosophers of this kind, and more recently Teilhard de Chardin used this method in a daring theological synthesis. There is *empiricism*, a standpoint which it is harder for theology to reach, although I. T. Ramsey has tried to show the meaning of religious language and commitment in an empirical context.[2] Thirdly there is *existentialism*, which places reality within man's self-understanding, so that propositions about God or about any ontological concept have no validity except as accounts of man's encounters. While the first two kinds of philosophy look out into the world to investigate it, the last withdraws from statements about the world to find reality in man's discovery of himself and his relationships and commitments.

It is not surprising that at a time when so many of the old securities of traditional thought are in confusion existentialism has been attractive to exponents of Christianity. The existentialist strain is, on any showing, strongly present within the New Testament writings. So often the assertions of the apostolic writers about God and Jesus and the world are assertions in terms of personal commitment. The confession that Jesus is Lord was a confession about the disciple himself in his submission to Jesus. The belief of the Christian in

[2] I. T. Ramsey, *Religious Language*, London: SCM Press; New York: Macmillan, 1957.

the resurrection of Jesus went with the will to die to sin, and instantly to know him as the centre of one's own life. If the belief in the Ascension passed beyond spatial terms into the conviction that Jesus was omnipresent and sovereign it was because of what the unseen Jesus meant to the believers in their own lives: it was that relationship which cut across spatial and metaphysical categories. Nowhere is the existential note more clear than in the dialogue between Jesus and Nicodemus. Nicodemus asks for information about the teaching and authority of Jesus and at once the ground is cut from beneath his feet by the demand 'except a man be born anew he cannot see the kingdom of God'.

II

IN BULTMANN demythologizing, which had from the beginning been a factor in the processes of Christian understanding, becomes the universal panacea, and existentialist theology becomes the universal answer. The whole New Testament revelation must undergo a whole translation into a whole theological method.

A pastoral and evangelistic passion inspired Bultmann. In the New Testament the records about Jesus and the preaching of the apostles are intermingled with the three-storied Ptolemaic universe and a world of angels, visions, miracles, demons, and the gospel of salvation is presented in terms of the Son of God descending from a local heaven and returning thither, soon to come again in weird happenings. To modern minds this world of thought is incredible and unacceptable, but there is a reality to which it was, in its own way, witnessing, and that reality must be given to the modern world to meet its desperate needs.

The old liberals had extracted from the mythological element in the New Testament what they supposed to be the real story of the teaching and example of Jesus. But this was a false procedure, for it was in the mythology that the apostolic interpretation of Jesus lay. The true answer, says Bultmann, is not to cut away the mythology but to conserve it whole and to *translate its meaning whole* to modern man.

What was the New Testament mythology, in its own way, saying? It was saying that man discovers his own existence in his encounter with the Faith-Event of Jesus. The Faith-Event is not the Crucifixion as an episode to be recorded historically, followed by the Resurrection as another episode recorded historically. It was the Crucifixion *as preached and believed*. The event is unknowable apart from the existentialist encounter of men with God in their acceptance of his word. The death of Jesus is known only as the believer's dying with Christ in the hearing of faith. The Resurrection is not an event which evidence attests: it is a mythological way of proclaiming the saving significance of the Cross; and all that the historian can affirm is the Easter faith of the disciples. The theology of the primitive Church was a clothing of the existential Gospel in various kinds of interpretative imagery. It was only after the Cross-Resurrection event that there came revelation, faith, Christology and the use of the various Messianic titles to express the apostles' belief.

In this total translation of the Gospel into existentialist terms Bultmann's thesis has radical consequences for theology and for history. For *theology* there is no room for ontological propositions about the status of Jesus in relation to God and the world. The doctrines of the Sonship or the Logos are not metaphysical statements but witnesses to the existential relationship of Jesus to the believer. For *history* there is something near to scepticism about the records of the life and teaching of Jesus.

In his book *Jesus and the Word*[3] Bultmann drew out powerfully the teaching of Jesus as the demand for radical obedience when the hearer is confronted with the immediacy of God. Jesus was a rabbi whose teaching made God overwhelmingly near and vivid; such was his authority. But there were no messianic claims or titles, no Christology, until after the Resurrection. Nor is his life before the Crucifixion either knowable or important. Writing near the beginning of the book Bultmann thus described its scope:

For the same reason, interest in the personality of Jesus

[3] The book was published in German with the title *Jesus* in 1926, and in England with the title *Jesus and the Word* in 1935 (London: Nicholson & Watson). Bultmann's view of the mission of Jesus is presented again in the first volume of his *Theology of the New Testament* (London: SCM Press; New York: Scribners, 1952). His view of demythologizing is summarized in his essay in *Kerygma and Myth*, ed. H. W. Bartsch (London: S.P.C.K., 1953).

is excluded [from this book] – and not merely because, in the absence of information, I am making a virtue of necessity. I do indeed think that we can now know almost nothing concerning the life and personality of Jesus, since the early Christian sources show no interest in either, are moreover fragmentary and often legendary; and other sources about Jesus do not exist.[4]

True, Jesus is far from insignificant: Jesus is 'the one in whom God's word encounters man, whatever titles are given to him'. This encounter implied a Christology, and the post-Resurrection Church was right to formulate one. But what sort of man was this Jesus through whom God encounters us? No processes of historical evidence are able to show us the answer, and it is wrong to ask, as the historical curiosity which would wish to discover a portrait of Jesus is a lapse into *historismus* from the pure attitude of faith.

Such is Bultmann's retranslation of the Gospel for the modern world. He shows us Jesus as the Divine Saviour, through whom men are justified by faith alone and liberated from the 'demonic' forces of fear, selfishness and the pressures of the world. God becomes meaningful in his encounter with man, and man becomes meaningful as he is delivered into the encounter with God. Here is the true doctrine of human existence.

But can theology stay where Bultmann leaves it, and is it the whole meaning of the New Testament which he translates? These questions at once arise.

First, it seems that Bultmann does no sort of justice

[4] *Jesus and the Word*, p. 14.

to the emphasis of the New Testament writers upon the
man Jesus. Let it be granted that the materials for a
biography of Jesus do not exist, and that history and
interpretation cannot be disentangled. None the less the
references to Jesus in the Epistles and the large space
given within the Gospel traditions to the deeds and
sayings of Jesus show that the Church was interested
not only in the fact that God encountered the human
race through someone's death but also in the character
of the man through whom this encounter took place.
The emphasis of St Luke upon the characteristics of the
humanity of Jesus, of the Epistle to the Hebrews upon
his human conflicts and of the First Epistle of St Peter
upon the example of Jesus which Christians must follow – all this has no place in the New Testament Christianity which Bultmann translates, and therefore no
place in his translation. The *imitatio Christi* disappears
from Christianity.

Next, Bultmann confuses the question of myth in the
New Testament before ever he sets out to demytholo-
gize. He regards the mythology of the New Testament
as a single frame based upon a Ptolemaic astronomy and
a deity who descends from heaven and ascends again.
But not all the myths in the New Testament fall into
that category, and the New Testament contains both
processes of demythologizing on its own account and
also symbolism which conveyed and still conveys truth
in a poetic way. The varieties of Christological imagery
are more than Bultmann allows. The imagery of 'up'
and 'down', 'above' and 'below' did not necessarily

imply literal topography in the Bible. It could convey
the distinctions of deity and humanity, creator and
creature, lord and servant, moral perfection and moral
imperfection. The problem of translation is not just that
the apostles thought entirely in a Ptolemaic imagery
and we do not. It is also, and perhaps still more,
that the apostles were trained in a religious poetical
expression and many modern minds think only in
prosy sophistications. Bultmann has oversimplified,
and thus misrepresented the complex character of
biblical language in the all-or-nothing of his sweeping
theory.

Lastly, while the existential element in the New
Testament has, as we saw, an important place, so that
an existential theology today is able to recapture it,
there is also an *ontological* element in the New Testament as utterly essential for New Testament Christianity. In the experience of salvation existentialism
may seem to suffice, for the Saviour is definable as
'what he means to me'. But in the experience of worship
the Christian was and is concerned with *One who is*.
The worshipper forgets his own being and experiences
in the adoration of One who is, and the 'isness' of deity
is there, behind and before, now and for ever. The
'isness' of deity – prominent in the Old Testament –
is reaffirmed when it is revealed that Jesus shares in it.
St John shows that the glory of Jesus which men encountered in his life and death is the glory of deity in
eternity. Is it that an exclusively Protestant view of
Christianity as the religion of the Word, which misses

the deep emphasis of Catholic Christianity upon adoration, causes Bultmann to suppose that an existentialist concept can convey the whole meaning of Christianity? Ontology, 'isness', 'being' is ineradicable from the Christianity of the New Testament.

In these ways Bultmann's translation of the Gospel from the first century to the twentieth is incomplete and even misleading. Yet his effort should evoke the gratitude of those who, learning both from his successes and his failures, can set out to find better translations of the Gospel to the modern world. Few have done more than Bultmann to challenge Christian thought to its tasks, with the constant reminder that while we study Christ it is Christ who judges us.

III

IT SEEMS fair to speak already of a 'post-Bultmann' era, for both in the study of the gospel history and in the development of philosophical theology there are those who, acknowledging their debt to Bultmann, have passed beyond the limitations which he created for himself.

In the study of the history of Jesus there are disciples of Bultmann who, accepting his view of the existential character of the Gospel, are concerned to fill his historical *lacuna* in the life of Jesus before the Crucifixion and believe that there is historical evidence enough to enable the *lacuna* to be filled.[5] An instance of this new historical

[5] A valuable pioneer work in dealing with this *lacuna* was

quest appeared in the work *Jesus of Nazareth* by Günther Bornkamm which was published in German in 1956 and in English in 1960. The author shows his debt to Bultmann when he writes:

To make the reality of God present, this is the essential mystery of Jesus. This making present of the reality of God signifies the end of the world in which it takes place.[6]

But for Bornkamm the challenge of divine immediacy which Jesus gave was inseparable from *what Jesus was really like* in his words and actions. The traditions allow us to know a good deal about what Jesus was really like in the variety of human situations with which he was confronted. In them he brought home the nearness and claim of God by a blending of authority and humility, of severity and compassion. A portrait of a person emerges from the records, and it was *that* person who made God near and real and it was *that* person who died on the Cross and justified the Christology of the early Church. In this way the life of Jesus gave both an historical prelude and a theological basis for what followed; and in elaborating this theme Bornkamm parts company with Bultmann, though he still follows him when he says:

The secret of his being could only reveal itself to the disciples in his resurrection.[7]

R. H. Fuller, *The Mission and Achievement of Jesus* (London: SCM Press, 1954), though the author has subsequently modified some of his conclusions.

[6] G. Bornkamm, *Jesus of Nazareth*, London: Hodder & Stoughton, 1960, p. 62.

[7] Ibid., p. 178.

In the next chapter I shall be discussing further the ways in which the gospel traditions afford evidence for a picture of the human figure of Jesus in relation to his contemporaries.

In philosophical theology also it is possible to speak of a 'post-Bultmann' development, and it seems already to augur well.

Dr John Macquarrie has distinguished two kinds of theological use of existentialism. There are

those whose interest in existentialism has been confined mainly to its analysis of man in his historical existence, and those who have moved beyond this towards an existentially based ontology.[8]

Bultmann is in the first of these categories, and for theism it is an unsure position as 'God's action upon me' does not entirely correspond with what the Bible means by 'I am that I am'. But in the second category, among those who pass on to an existentially-based ontology, Macquarrie himself appears as a creative exponent. His massive work, *Principles of Christian Theology*,[9] is a readable, lucid and moving presentation of the pattern of Christian doctrine in 'existentialist-ontological' terms.

In this great work Macquarrie contends that theism is properly to be expounded not in terms of God as *a being* amongst other beings but in terms of *Being*. The proposition 'God exists' is valid as equivalent to speaking

[8] J. Macquarrie, *God and Secularity*, p. 97; cf. his *Studies in Christian Existentialism*, London: SCM Press, 1965.
[9] New York: Scribners, 1966; London: SCM Press, 1967.

of the *Holiness of Being*. To speak thus is to draw a very clear line between theism and atheism. God's relation to the world is one of Being expressed in Let-Being; and in terms of Let-Being Macquarrie impressively draws out the doctrine of the Trinity and the meaning of creation. Thence the theme passes on to the Incarnation and the redeeming work of Christ. While the starting-point of the exposition of Christian doctrine is, for the author, seen in existentialist terms, it is an ontological Christianity which emerges, a Christianity which includes not only 'what God does for me' but the adoration of the Triune God and the sacrament of the Eucharist as the key to the Christian meaning of the natural order. The debt of Macquarrie's exposition to the creative impulse of existentialist thinking is none the less for its passing far beyond existentialism in its presentation of the doctrine of the Triune God.

A word in conclusion about myth and symbol. If we reject, as I think we should, Bultmann's simple solution, it remains true that we are always involved with myth and symbol and their role in Christian theology and worship. Here is an instance of the confusion caused by faulty thinking about the literal and the symbolical. The well-known hymn for Palm Sunday includes the lines:

> The Father on his sapphire throne
> Expects his own anointed Son.

What confusion is here! The scene in the hymn is one of plain historical fact. Jesus is riding on an ass through the streets of Jerusalem. But 'the Father on his sapphire throne' is symbolism, akin to that of the Book of Revelation: it symbolizes the paternity and sovereignty of God. Abruptly to confuse the literal and symbolical in this way is to create hurtful unintelligibility. Are those who sing the hymn to think of Jesus riding through the streets on an ass with a Father on a throne to greet him at the end of the ride? It not seldom happens that young children become very confused by Christian teaching in which symbolic pictures and historical facts are confused, and disillusion may come later when a kind of fairy-land of belief is disturbed. Imaginative symbol, historical fact and prose definition all have their place in the apprehension of the truth of God. For the sake of young and old alike their roles must be distinguished.

FOUR

Jesus in History

THE MODERN reader of the gospels is puzzled by the question of their historical value. How far do they give a record of what really happened? How far may theology or symbolism obscure the factual record? The degree to which the reader will feel this of course varies. To one the presence of wonder stories and angels and demons in the narrative seems hard to reconcile with his idea of historical probability. To another the theological colouring which recurs in the narratives may arouse the suspicion that it belongs to some *motif* of the writers rather than to the original story. But quite apart from such particular critical viewpoints the reader will notice the discrepancies in the narratives which are enough to show that every detail cannot be literally true. It cannot be true both that the sons of Zebedee made an improper request for the chief seats in the day of glory and that their mother made the request instead of them. It cannot be true that the anointing at Bethany was both in the house of Lazarus and in the house of Simon the leper, or that the last supper was both the Passover meal and the meal on the eve of the Passover. Jesus may have said 'Why do you call me good? No one is good except God' to the rich young man, or he may have said 'Why do you ask me about what is good?'; but the two remarks are not identical.

C

Now the problem has been the subject of the immense labours of historical and literary criticism for more than a century, and the story of those labours cannot be told again here. The supreme question has been: how much about Jesus do we really know to be true? And it is now possible to distinguish two contrasted ways of answering the question. The one way, initiated by the historical criticism of the last century, was to try to construct from within the gospel traditions the original 'plain' factual story of Jesus as distinct from the theological, ecclesiastical and supernatural interpretations supposed to be read into the story by the post-Resurrection Church. The other way, initiated by the form-critics in the second and third decades of the present century, is to suggest that it is impossible to separate fact and interpretation in the older manner, that fact and interpretation belong together in every phase of the gospel traditions, and that the gospels give us an interpretative portrait of Jesus which may take us very near to the actual events if the interpretation was in fact a true one.

II

IT IS worth recalling the older phase of the study of the history of Jesus both for its own virtues and for the sake of seeing the newer phase in perspective. The 'liberal' lives of Jesus written in the last century set out to portray the simple facts in contrast with the supernaturalizing and theologizing imported into the story by the early Church. The attempt was deeply influenced by certain presuppositions: that the miraculous is incredible as it conflicts with the uniformity of nature and is to be rejected as unhistorical or explained away; that the original story and message of Jesus were 'simple', and 'simple' meant congruous with the ethical ideals of nineteenth-century liberal thought.[1] In this way the liberal lives solved the problem of the gospels by a dichotomy, ascribing history to the life of Jesus and supernaturalism to the beliefs of the early Church.

The long reign of the liberal lives of Jesus was broken by two happenings. The first was the influence of Albert Schweitzer. His book *Von Reimarus zu Wrede*, published in 1906 and known to the English-speaking world by the title *The Quest of the Historical Jesus*,[2] saw as the heart and centre of the message of Jesus the apocalyptic element which the liberal lives had banished as too bizarre to be historical. Few indeed came to accept Schweitzer's thesis in its neat wholeness – that Jesus's message was to proclaim the imminence of the end and that his moral teaching was a set of interim ethics for the months or weeks that still remained – for Schweitzer built very much upon a single text, Matthew 10.23,

[1] Tyrrell's well-known description of Harnack's picture of Jesus as the reflection of a Liberal Protestant face at the bottom of a deep well has recently been matched by Professor Dennis Nineham's comment on some nineteenth-century lives of Jesus: 'A fairly close correlation could be observed between a particular writer's picture and his general views on social and religious questions' (D. Nineham, 'Jesus in the Gospels' in *Christ for Us Today*, ed. Norman Pittenger, London: SCM Press, 1968, p. 51).

[2] London: A. & C. Black, 1910.

'You will not have gone through the towns of Israel before the Son of Man comes.' But Schweitzer struck a blow, almost indeed a death-blow, to the idea that Jesus must be easily intelligible to the modern world, and showed that Jesus and his message were strange, catastrophic and otherworldly, no less challenging to modern ethical idealism than to the ideas of his contemporaries in Palestine. It came to be accepted by students of the gospels that eschatology, in some sense or other, belonged to the essence of the message of Jesus.[3]

The other development which damaged the dominance of the liberal lives was the coming of scholarly investigations of the gospels and their sources which showed that the 'liberal' interpretation was arbitrary, inasmuch as the earlier, no less than the later, strata of the written traditions behind the gospels contain messianic and supernatural claims and the germs of the Christology of the apostolic age. It may suffice here to recall the revered names of E. C. Hoskyns in England and B. S. Easton in America. Both of these scholars had a notable share in demonstrating that the earliest literary sources in the gospels show Jesus not only as a teacher and prophet but as the bringer of messianic salvation.[4]

[3] For an assessment of the influence of Schweitzer I would refer to my work *From Gore to Temple*, London: Longmans, 1960, pp. 171–175.

[4] Cf. E. C. Hoskyns, 'The Christ of the Synoptic Gospels' in *Essays Catholic and Critical*, London: S.P.C.K., 1926, and (with F. N. Davey) *The Riddle of the New Testament*, London: Faber, 1931; B. S. Easton, *The Gospel before the Gospels*, New York: Scribners, 1929.

Yet all through the phase of gospel studies which we have been describing it was supposed that, given the right critical procedures, it was possible to find in the gospels material of a more or less *biographical* kind. St Mark's Gospel was commonly read as a collection of St Peter's memories of the life of Jesus with a chronological plan, and it was supposed that motives of a biographical kind largely accounted for the labours of the evangelists. I would illustrate this by two quotations from F. C. Burkitt's work *The Gospel History and its Transmission*, a work which long had immense influence:

> It is the peculiar merit of St Mark's Gospel, from the point of view of historical investigation, that it deals mainly with a cycle of events foreign to the life and interests of the Christian communities.[5]

> The other gospels, even the Gospel according to Matthew and Luke, give us an interpretation of Jesus Christ's life. An interpretation may be helpful, illuminating, even inspired, but it remains an interpretation. The thing that actually occurred is the life that Jesus Christ lived, and our chief authority for that life is the Gospel according to St Mark.[6]

In the rigid distinction between fact and interpretation, and in the view of St Mark's Gospel as a kind of photographic record, these words of Burkitt seem very far from the newer phase in the study of the gospels. It is perhaps a half-conscious adherence to the earlier

[5] F. C. Burkitt, *The Gospel History and its Transmission*, Edinburgh: T. & T. Clark, 1906, p. 61.
[6] Ibid., p. 103.

assumptions which has made the newer phase difficult
for some devout people to grasp today.

III

IT WAS the emergence of Form-Criticism which radically altered the scene of gospel studies. Starting from
the time of the 1914–18 World War with the work of
Martin Dibelius, K. L. Schmidt, Rudolf Bultmann and
others, the new school used the gospel traditions first
of all as evidence for the form and content of the teaching about Jesus given in the early Christian communities.
Before the gospels were written there were several
decades in which the traditions about Jesus were
handed down in oral tradition, and we can detect
within the gospels the various 'forms' in which the
stories about Jesus and his teaching were told. Inevitably the tradition would come to be shaped by the
Church's many didactic, liturgical and apologetic
needs, and those who narrated the traditions in the
Christian communities would present them not in a
biographical shape but in relation to the Church's
current needs. Such was the background to the eventual
writing of the gospels, and with that background the
evangelists would seem to have written not biographies
of Jesus so much as collections of episodes from the
Church's traditions about Jesus with a view to showing how the Gospel of God came into the world through
his life, deeds, words, death and resurrection. The
material was indeed biographical material, but the

motive and plan were 'kerygmatic' rather than biographical and coloured by the Church's theology and
worship.

If the gospels were written from the background and
with the motives which Form-Criticism describes, are
we sure that they give us reliable factual history? Do
they tell us what really happened?

In dealing with this question some of the exponents
of Form-Criticism have used their science for the making of somewhat negative historical judgements and
have been over-ready to assure us that this or that
element in a gospel narrative is a non-historical im-
portation from the post-Resurrection Church. T. W.
Manson, who held that Form-Criticism exceeded its
function when it made judgements about historical
criticism, wrote trenchantly:

We can list these stories in the gospels. We can label
them and other units when we are agreed about the
terminology of the science. But a paragraph of Mark is not
a penny the better or the worse as historical evidence for
being labelled pronouncement, story or paradigm.[7]

I do not, however, think that those words of Manson
do justice to the issue. Form-Criticism cannot make

[7] T. W. Manson, 'The Life of Jesus: some tendencies in present-
day research' in *The Background of the New Testament and its
Eschatology*, Cambridge University Press, 1956, p. 212. A somewhat rigid scheme of canons for deciding the historicity of the
sayings of Jesus is, I think, a fault in R. H. Fuller's admirable
book *The Foundations of New Testament Christology*, London:
Lutterworth Press, 1965. He even speaks of 'the rules of traditio-
historical criticism', p. 111.

historical judgements for us, but it can help us to see the setting in which the gospels were written and the nature of the historical question at stake. We need to ask how the history concerning Jesus was originally thought of in relation to the Church's interpretation of it, and what kind of historical certainty is under the circumstances possible.

What, then, was the place of the historical life of Jesus within the thought of the early Christians? Certainly the early Christians were immensely interested in what Jesus had done and taught in his earthly life. Certainly, also, the Christians had plenty of access to the information about him through the presence of eyewitnesses and the apostles whom he had commissioned. The Christians cared about the history and were able to know much about it, and it was of vital concern for them and for the world. But the nature of their interest was, through the circumstances of early Christianity, very different from, for instance, that of the author and the readers of Xenophon's *Memorabilia* or of Plutarch's *Lives*.

First, the Christians believed that the Jesus whose history they cherished was alive in the midst of his Church and still teaching his people through the Holy Spirit and still feeding them with the Bread of Life. The life of Jesus in Palestine up to the Crucifixion was thus, in the mind of the Church, but one chapter in a continuing drama; and the stories about Jesus in the days of his flesh were now cherished as a part of a still continuing act. Therefore, in the Church's use of the traditions about Jesus in Palestine, there might be a blurring of the distinction between past and present, between fact and interpretation, between the setting of Palestine and the setting of the post-Resurrection Church. I find the matter understood in this way by Professor D. E. Nineham in his well-known *Penguin Commentary on St Mark*. In that Commentary, though some of the particular judgements on points of history are more 'sceptical' than I should find necessary, I do not feel that the general line is a sceptical one, for the author sees the history of Jesus as supremely important for the early Church though important as the first chapter of his continuing life.

Secondly, the first Christians believed that in the events concerning Jesus there had been a unique action of God in history, supernatural in its relation to the historical order and bringing salvation to the world. In telling the story of the Man Jesus they were telling of what God was doing, and the story was in their minds a story about heaven as well as about earth. How would they bring out this aspect of the history? Not by adding theological propositions as rubrics in the narrative, but by the use of familiar religious symbols. And references to the presence of angels, to the skies opening, to a voice from heaven or to God speaking to someone 'in a dream' were perhaps a way of saying 'this was God's doing'. If, therefore, a symbolic element of this kind came into the traditions as an accompaniment and interpretation of the history, the evangelists would be like their own times if they did not themselves distinguish between actual fact and symbolic accompaniment.

The upshot is that to read the gospels in the 'new' way which Form-Criticism has brought about is not necessarily to reduce their historical value for the life of Jesus, but rather to re-present that historical value, not in terms of the photographic reminiscences cherished by F. C. Burkitt and others of his generation, but in terms of an interpretative portrait which may none the less be a true portrait if the interpretation is a true one.

What are the features of that portrait? The procedure for discovering it was described thus by C. H. Dodd in his *History and the Gospel*:

. . . a method of criticism which promises a fresh approach to the problem of historicity. It is a method which does not aim directly or in the main at establishing a residuum of bare facts presumed to stand independently of any meaning attached to them . . . the aim is to recover the purest and most original form of the tradition which inevitably includes both fact and interpretation.[8]

We find a similar approach in Professor Nineham's *St Mark*:

As we have seen, it is possible to some extent to reconstruct the units of tradition on which the gospels are based. When we do reconstruct them, not only do we find that the units on which St Mark is based presuppose *broadly* the same Christ as the finished Gospel, but we

[8] C. H. Dodd, *History and the Gospel*, London: Nisbet, 1938, p. 103.

find that other units, preserved independently in other places and used by the other evangelists, also preserve a fundamentally similar figure. Our basic picture of Christ is thus carried back to a point only a quarter of a century or so after his death; and when we bear in mind the wonderfully retentive memory of the Oriental, who, being unable to read and write, had perforce to cultivate accuracy of memory, it will not seem surprising that we can often be virtually sure that what the tradition is offering us are the authentic deeds, and especially the authentic words, of the historic Jesus.[9]

Using the method described Dodd asked what were the features of the portrait of Jesus widely attested by a consensus of the traditions about his actions, relationships, sayings and parables, and he gave this result:

1. Jesus's compassionate searching for the outcasts of society.
2. Jesus's loneliness, separated by his vocation from home and family.
3. Jesus is in victorious conflict with supernatural powers of evil which assault many sufferers, his disciples and himself.
4. Jesus by his presence in the world marks the line between the old order and the new.
5. Jesus is the fulfilment of the anticipations and hopes contained in the Old Testament.
6. Jesus brings divine judgement upon the nation.[10]

I would not hesitate to add to the list, using the same scientific principles:

[9] D. Nineham, op. cit., pp. 50–51.
[10] C. H. Dodd, op. cit., pp. 91–103.

1. Jesus, whatever other titles he uses or rejects, speaks of a sonship of himself to the Father, intimate and not identical with the general sonship of the disciples.
2. Jesus predicts his own death, not as a disaster but as lying within the kingdom of God.
3. Jesus predicts beyond his death a divine vindication expressed in a variety of images.
4. Jesus summons his followers to die with him so as to share in the vindication. It will be a vindication of himself, of them, and perhaps of the human race ('Son of Man') with him.

The portrait is not the portrait of one whose biography can be constructed, though some of its episodes can with fair confidence be set in a sequence of before and after. It is an existentialist figure whom we are shown, one who challenges human existence with the divine judgement and the divine generosity. But it is also a real, visible, human figure, who challenges men not just as a kind of *incognito* within whom deity is veiled but as one who can be known in and for himself and loved and imitated.[11]

It is, therefore, fair to say that the methods of Form-Criticism do not deprive us of having considerable

[11] When we speak about a new quest of the historical Jesus we should pay heed to two warnings given in different contexts by Professor Nineham. To concentrate *exclusively* on the historical material would be false to the total interests of the New Testament; cf. *Historicity and Chronology in the New Testament*, London: S.P.C.K., 1965, p. 16. To over-modernize Jesus is a fault already apparent in the new quest as in the former quest; cf. *Christ for Us Today*, p. 56.

knowledge of Jesus as an historical figure. Further-more, while Form-Criticism encourages us in the main to read the gospels in the perspective of the post-Resurrection Christian communities, it remains note-worthy that not a few signs of the pre-Crucifixion perspective survive in the synoptic traditions. For in-stance, the teaching of Jesus about the law and about his own relation to the Gentiles seems to belong to the initial stage of the sowing of seeds rather than to the final stage of the Church's realization. And the sayings of Jesus about the Holy Spirit do not suggest a reading-back of the Church's developed theology. So, too, there are incidents whose telling seems to conserve the memory of what happened irrespective of didactic or apologetic value. There is no more arbitrary hypothesis than that the Church was uninterested in remembering and relating *what Jesus was like*.

IV

THE ENTIRE theme of this chapter would, however, collapse were it not for the Resurrection of Jesus. Without the Resurrection the Christian movement would have petered out in ignominy and there would have been no Christianity. It is not too much to say that without the Resurrection the phenomenon of Christianity in the apostolic age and since is scientifi-cally unaccountable. It is also true to say that without the Resurrection Christianity would not be itself, as the distinctiveness of Christianity is not its adherence to a teacher who lived long ago but its belief that 'Jesus is Lord' for every generation through the centuries.

The Resurrection is something which 'happened' a few days after the death of Jesus. The apostles became convinced that Jesus was alive and that God had raised him to life. It is not historically scientific to say only that the apostles came to realize the divine meaning of the Crucifixion for them or that the person of Jesus now became contagious to them. Something *happened* so as to vindicate for them the meaning of the Cross, and to make the person of Jesus contagious to them. The evidence for a stupendous happening, which the New Testament writers mention, was the survival of the Church, the appearances of Jesus in a visible and audible impact on the apostles, and the discovery that the tomb was empty. The several elements in this threefold evidence no doubt had different degrees of evidential weight for different people, and they have such varying degrees still. As to significance, if it were the existential encounter of Jesus which alone mattered, then the empty tomb would have little or no significance. If, however, Jesus has a *cosmic* meaning with cosmic effects then the empty tomb has great significance, akin to the significance of the Incarnation itself.

Undoubtedly the Resurrection faith was in one aspect existential. The belief of the apostles that Jesus had been raised from death was different from the decision of a jury that an event had happened on the basis of certain evidences. The apostles' belief was bound up with their response to Christ as living and with his impact upon them. As St Paul told the Corinthians, if Christ had not been raised they were still in their sins, but they had known the Resurrection as issuing in their passage from their sins into a new realm of conduct. But, *pace* Bultmann, there was another side to the process of belief. The apostles, for all the existential character of the Easter faith, were yet at pains to confirm to themselves and to others that it was a reasonable faith and that there were facts inexplicable apart from the Resurrection. There was not only the challenge of the existential encounter: there was also the challenge of evidence, the challenge to explain a number of events and experiences other than by the Resurrection. That was the significance of the catena of evidence cited by St Paul in I Corinthians 15, of the inclusion of the particular Easter stories within the tradition and of the collections of stories made by the evangelists. The Emmaus story illustrates the various ingredients in belief in the Resurrection. There was the climax, Jesus known and recognized in the breaking of the bread and vanishing from their sight: it was the moment of faith and encounter. But there had been previously the reflection on the divine purpose in the scriptures which the stranger had unfolded to them on the road. There had been the report that the tomb had been found empty, and that the discovery had been corroborated by other observers. There was the corroboration of the two disciples' seeing of Jesus at Emmaus by the news that the apostles in Jerusalem had also seen him.

I am suggesting not that the Emmaus story tells us

exactly how the Easter faith began, but that it illustrates the apostolic Church's view of the factors in the creation of that faith for the original and subsequent believers. To value these evidential factors is not, as Bultmann suggests, to lapse into a worldly-minded historicism, for the Easter faith, existential as it is, was and is related to evidential history. Christians believe in the Resurrection partly because a series of facts are unaccountable without it.

Because of the Resurrection the Church survived so as to hand down the traditions about Jesus, and in consequence we know not a little about Jesus and his life and teaching. But that knowledge was conserved because of the significance for humanity which Jesus was believed to possess. It is now for us to ask what that significance was, and is.

FIVE

Jesus, God and Man

THE EARLIEST Christian Creed was the statement 'Jesus is Lord' and it is still the core of Christian belief. I invite my readers now to consider the origin of that belief in the light of New Testament studies, and the implications of that belief for the understanding of God and man.

The question which Jesus posed to his followers was 'Who do you say that I am?', and the question posed through many centuries has been 'Is Jesus divine?' Those questions assume that the concepts of God and of man are initially meaningful and that the query is how to relate Jesus to those concepts. Today, however, it is more often being asked whether God is meaningful and whether man is intelligible. It is, therefore, for Christians to concern themselves not only with the assertion of the deity of Jesus but with the claim that Jesus shows the meaningfulness of God and the intelligibility of man.

I

IT IS clear from the synoptic gospels that the theme of the preaching and teaching of Jesus was the kingdom of God. He picked up a central theme of the Old Testament, that God's sovereignty is an eternal fact, that it is now contradicted by the morally rebellious state of the world, and that one day it will be vindicated in history by a great divine intervention, 'the coming of the kingdom of God'. Jesus comes into Galilee proclaiming that the reign of God is imminent, or is indeed breaking here and now into history: 'The time is fulfilled, and the kingdom of God is at hand; repent and believe in the gospel' (Mark 1.15).

The kingdom of God is made near and challenging by the works of Jesus and by his teaching of righteousness. Together the works and the righteousness are parts of a new order which Jesus is bringing into the world, the assertion of the divine sovereignty in the life of man. To welcome only the physical benefits brought by Jesus in his works of healing and other miracles is to mistake the nature of the new order in which the new righteousness with its gift and its demand is central.

What is the righteousness of the kingdom? It is not a code of law, though it does imply and include law – the old divine law reaffirmed in terms of a deeper principle of obedience in heart and motive. The essence of the ethics of Jesus is not law, but a relationship of persons to God. They are to live their lives towards God, sensitive to his nearness and goodness and, through this sensitivity, they will find themselves reflecting his character and possessed by his goodness. It is the ethics of a Godward relationship. Thus men are to *love* their enemies as well as their friends, reflecting the indiscriminate goodness of God who gives rain and sunshine to good and bad alike. Again, one of the root

evils in human life is fear, the soil in which self-concern
and defensive self-interest can grow: but live with sensitivity to God's goodness, who cares for the lilies and
clothes the fields with grass, and *faith* replaces fear and
the sins of which fear is the parent. Again, men will
forgive one another, reflecting towards others the un-
deserved divine forgiveness of themselves for what they
have done and not done.

So the righteousness of Jesus is the righteousness of a
Godward relationship of trust, dependence, receptivity.
It is a terribly hard kind of righteousness. It is sometimes hard because it involves the calls of sacrifice and
self-renunciation which Jesus gives. But it is more often
hard because of the shattering generosity of God, de-
manding an utterly childlike receptivity. To receive like
a little child an unmerited gift and to be humbled in the
receiving time and time again: such is the righteousness
of the kingdom. It follows that in Christian ethics humility has a continuing place which throughout history
secular forms of ethics find very hard to understand.
It also follows that St Paul's teaching about justifica-
tion by faith, the doctrine of being right with God on the
basis of God's own gift, is in a true line with the ethics of
Jesus.

But the kingdom is here, as Jesus speaks of it. To
enter it or to receive it (both phrases recur) is to look
not towards a general concept of deity but towards a
specific divine activity happening instantly and ur-
gently in the presence, the works and the teaching of
Jesus. God is doing something. A new order is here.

The time is fulfilled (Mark 1.15), prophets and kings
had longed to see what the followers of Jesus are now
seeing (Matt. 13.16–17; Luke 10.23–24), something
greater than Jonah, greater than Solomon is here
(Matt. 12.41–42; Luke 11.31–32). And it is the presence of Jesus doing what he does and saying what
he says which marks the new order. His presence
casting out devils shows the presence of the kingdom of God (Matt. 12.28; Luke 11.20). John the
Baptist, the greatest of men yet born, is less than the
least who has found his way within the kingdom (Matt.
11.11).

So it is that, amidst the self-effacement with which
Jesus makes not himself but the kingdom his message
and his entire absorption, the implied claims concerning his own relation to the kingdom are far-reaching.
It will be in terms of their relation to Jesus that men will
face a final judgement, and it will be Jesus who will
accept or reject them (Matt. 7.21–22). The self-renunciation demanded of Jesus's followers is to be made for
the sake of Jesus (Mark 10.29), and the future reward
will be glory *with him* (Mark 10.37). Meanwhile his
death will be the ground of a new covenant relation between God and men (Mark 14.24). Finally, there are
sayings of Jesus which give more than a hint of the
underlying secret: a unique sonship of Jesus to the
Father. True, Jesus is never described in the synoptic
gospels as calling himself by the title 'Son of God' or
'Son'; indeed the title by itself might convey very inadequate meaning to his hearers. The point is rather that

the evidence is strong that Jesus spoke in such a way as to distinguish his own sonship from the sonship of the disciples or of all men in general. It is 'my Father' and it is 'your Father'. The striking saying in Matthew 11.27 and Luke 10.22 about the unique relation of the Son to the Father, which used to be called 'the Johannine thunderbolt in the synoptic sky', is congruous with the evidence of other sayings.

The total picture is one in which a sort of egoism ('It was said of them of old time . . . but I say unto you') is blended with the self-effacement of a Son absorbed not in himself but in his Father. Jesus is a teacher of immense authority unable to define that authority because it is not his own and no verbal definitions will define it. 'There is,' says Bishop John Robinson, 'a paradox running through all the gospels that Jesus makes no claim for himself *in his own right*, and at the same time makes the most stupendous claims about what God is doing through him and uniquely through him.'[1] This paradox is still found in the Fourth Gospel where the glory of Jesus is not a glory of his own but a glory of self-giving love in dependence on the Father: 'If I glorify myself my glory is nothing' (John 8.54).

It is, therefore, not in the titles used by Jesus or ascribed to Jesus that the highest significance of his person is seen. Critical scholars have had much debate as

[1] J. A. T. Robinson, *Honest to God*, London: SCM Press, 1963, p. 73. Cf. C. K. Barrett, *Jesus and the Gospel Tradition*, London: S.P.C.K.; Philadelphia: Fortress Press, 1968, pp. 30–35.

to whether the titles – Son of Man, Son of God, Messiah, Lord – were *first* brought into the traditions of the sayings of Jesus by the post-Resurrection Church, though there is greater readiness to believe that the title Son of Man belongs to authentic sayings of Jesus.[2] But no titles were adequate to the nature of Jesus's authority. Did he accept the name of Messiah or Christ? Certainly Jesus did and said things appropriate to one who was Messiah, and his enemies set out to destroy him because his behaviour added up to a claim to Messiahship and more.

But if he accepted the title on the occasion of Peter's confession at Caesarea Philippi he at once overshadowed its meaning by predicting his death. He *may* have been accepting it by implication when he rode into the city of Jerusalem on an ass's colt (cf. Zech. 9.9). But the only occasion when the synoptists record him as avowing Messiahship was in his reply to the High Priest in the Sanhedrin when he was at the point of condemnation to death. And there, as elsewhere, he turned to the title Son of Man which he used in his teaching sometimes in connection with the necessity of suffering and sometimes in connection with vindication in glory afterwards;

---

[2] Amongst recent works R. H. Fuller, in *The Foundations of New Testament Christology*, London: Lutterworth Press, 1965, regards the use of messianic titles by Jesus as a reading of post-Resurrection formulae into the traditions; M. D. Hooker, in *The Son of Man in Mark*, London: S.P.C.K., 1967, concludes that Jesus used that title in his teaching; and C. K. Barrett, in *Jesus and the Gospel Tradition*, is 'conservative' about the title 'Son of Man', though not so about other titles.

and it is not certain how far he was speaking, by this title, of himself alone or of himself and his followers, or indeed of humanity as a whole passing with him through suffering to glory.

When, however, the necessity of his own suffering and death came into view Jesus so predicted his own suffering and death as to make it clear that they would be not a catastrophic defeat but part and parcel of his divine mission. What was in one aspect a crime plotted by the enemies of Jesus was in another aspect a mighty divine work to be wrought through him. It was necessary (Mark 8.31, 9.31, 10.34). Its necessity was of a divine purpose in the scriptures (Mark 14.21, 49). It would be a means of deliverance to 'many' (Mark 10.45). It would be the basis of a new covenant in his sacrificial blood (Mark 14.24). Small wonder that the old concepts about kingdom, messiahship, kingship were insufficient instruments for what Jesus was revealing, if the heart and the climax of the mission was an ignominious death. That death, however, was of the essence of that for which he had come, and the heart of his mission and his authority.

Beyond the death – what? In the event there happened the Resurrection and the emergence of Christianity, a faith within which the death was and is understood in terms not of defeat but of victorious sacrifice and self-giving love. Meanwhile the death was ignominious and an apparent defeat and disaster. C. K. Barrett has recently argued that Jesus died in disappointment, as two expectations had not been fulfilled – the expectation that the apostles would be with him to the last and die with him, the expectation that at the last there would be a divine intervention and 'a coming of the Son of Man'.[3] It may be that the grief and dereliction in the suffering of Jesus included that which Barrett describes, but I think that any such 'psychologizing' about the Gospel history lacks clear historical evidence one way or the other. The sayings of Jesus refer to a future vindication beyond the Cross, and a variety of images is used to express this, especially the imagery of a rising on the third day, and the imagery of the coming of the Son of Man in glory.

The apostles had been summoned by Jesus to share with him in his death as the precondition of sharing in the glory to come (Mark 8.34). None of the followers of Jesus died with him there and then. But subsequently the Christian life was presented in teaching, worship and theology as the sharing by Christians in Christ's death by a death-to-self, by a living-through-dying as the principle of daily existence, whether or not martyrdom was literally their lot. That was the meaning of Baptism (cf. Rom. 6.1–11) and the meaning of the Eucharist (Mark 14.23–24) as the feeding on the body and blood of Jesus. It was this understanding of the Christian life which lay behind St Luke's addition of the word 'daily' to the saying of Jesus about taking up the Cross (Luke 9.23).

[3] Cf. C. K. Barrett, *Jesus and the Gospel Tradition*, pp. 46–50, 84–86, 106–107.

II

SUCH WERE the foundations, within the life and teaching of Jesus, of the apostolic confession 'Jesus is Lord'.
The Resurrection vindicated the divine significance of
the Crucifixion and enabled the followers of Jesus to
understand what they had not understood before.
But the Resurrection could not of itself create the apostolic confession. It was not the Resurrection of 'X', it
was the Resurrection of Jesus whose life and teaching
had already made their impact.

The conviction of the Lordship of Jesus had come to
the apostles by way of their own reflection upon the
words and actions of Jesus, and Jesus had in his teaching encouraged thought, reflection, the asking of questions and the energy of judgement and conscience.
But it was no less a God-given belief, as St Paul says in
his uncompromising words: 'No one can say Jesus is
Lord except through the Holy Spirit' (I Cor. 12.3).

The attitude of the Church towards Jesus was becoming more than ardent devotion to a human teacher and
leader; it was becoming an attitude of faith and worship
towards one in whom were the characteristics of deity,
one believed to be supreme for the life of man and of
the world. Hence amidst their missionary labours some
of the apostolic company found themselves already
wrestling with the problems of thought about the understanding of Jesus in relation to God and the world.[4]

[4] Cf. R. H. Fuller, *The Foundations of New Testament Christology*, for the stages of belief and phraseology in the apostolic

In this process titles and images, for all their inadequacy, had their place. What should Jesus be called?
The title Lord, *kurios*, could have different tones and
undertones in different contexts. It could mean one with
sovereign power, with little more explicit definition. It
could mean the Messiah. It could mean – in the context
of the Greek cults – the Lord of a mystery religion. It
could recall the title used in the worship of the Roman
Emperor, *dominus noster*. It could mean, to readers of
the Greek Old Testament, the LORD God of the Bible.
Christos was a title quickly picked up and used in the
primitive Jewish Church, and now that the idea of
Messiahship had been revolutionized by the death of
Jesus it became fair to call him Messiah or Christ without any inhibition. But as the Church passed into the
Gentile world, where Hebrew ideas had little currency,
Christos tended to become a proper name for Jesus
rather than a title. As for 'Son' or 'Son of God', there
were contexts in which the title could mean no more
than an inspired man or one of the many demi-gods of
the pagan world. Nor in a biblical context was the meaning free from ambiguity, or inadequacy for the Church's
new-found faith. Hence in the Epistles significance
belongs not to the title itself so much as to the intimacy
with which it was used – 'his own son' (Rom. 8.32),
'his beloved Son' (Col. 1.13). It is in the Johannine

---

age. Cf. also John Knox, *The Humanity and Divinity of Christ*,
A Study of Pattern in Christology, Cambridge University Press,
1967.

writers that we see the title used with a metaphysical depth, implied as it was in the tradition of Jesus's unique intimacy with the Father. Every title used in revelation can mislead as well as reveal, for no words are adequate for the revelation. It is in the history of their use that their transcendent significance is seen.

No less significant than titles were the modes of thought which grew within the Church about the relation of Jesus to God. Five principal modes of thought appear. They may overlap and interpenetrate one another, but they are recognizable as what we may term the main types of emerging Christology.

1. Jesus who had lived and died was 'made Lord and Christ' at the Resurrection (Acts 2.36; cf. Rom. 1.4). This doctrine appears in the early days of the Church in Jerusalem. It is sometimes called the 'adoptionist' view. But that phrase needs to be used with caution. It was not that a man by his obedience attained a divine status. Such metaphysical ideas would be foreign to the minds of St Peter and his colleagues in Jerusalem. The point was rather that by the Resurrection Jesus became Messiah in full sovereignty, and the seal of divine significance was placed upon his history.

2. It was through Jesus in his life, death and Resurrection that God was uniquely present and active for the salvation of the world. It is a doctrine of divine presence and action throughout the events. God was in Christ reconciling the world to himself (II Cor.

5.19). God commends his own love to mankind in the death of Jesus (Rom. 5.8).

3. The Son of God pre-existed before his earthly life began, and was born into the world as man to be the Saviour. The imagery belongs both to St Paul and to St John, and it includes the coming of the Son into the world, the sending of the Son into the world, the giving of the Son, the self-emptying of the Son, the becoming poor of One who was rich. In these images the events of the Gospel are seen not only in the perspective of history but in the perspective of God's relations to the world. To use a human simile, there was a giving in the heart of eternal God in the birth, life, death and Resurrection of Jesus.

4. Jesus is the perfect mirror in humanity of what God is like. He reveals God fully. This is the 'symbolic' doctrine of his divinity, seen in the phrases 'the image of the invisible God' (Col. 1.15), the 'shining of tne glory of God' (Heb. 1.3) and in the sentence 'He who has seen me has seen the Father' (John 14.9).

5. Finally, there is the teaching of St John's prologue:

In the beginning was the Word, and the Word was with God, and the Word was God. . . . All things were made through him. . . . In him was life, and the life was the light of men. . . . The true light that enlightens every man was coming into the world. . . . And the Word became flesh and dwelt among us, full of grace and truth, and we have beheld his glory (John 1.1–14).

St John's imagery sets the fact of Jesus in a cosmic setting. The divine Word has been at work in the world ceaselessly, in creation, in the processes of nature and history, giving life to mankind and illuminating human minds with truth. Now comes the climax. In Jesus the divine Word is fully and finally revealed. While this final act is the goal of the divine energy at work through nature and history, it is also an act of self-giving by One who is beyond history, the Word, the creator, divine.

The Johannine prologue thus shows Jesus as the fulfilment of the divine within history, and also as an action from 'without'. 'Word', the term denotes One who is imperishable, the creator. 'Flesh', the term denotes humanity in its creatureliness, frailty, mortality. And St John is saying that One who is divine and the creator by an act in history takes upon himself the life of humanity in its creatureliness and frailty. *That* is what Christianity means by the Incarnation. It is a belief which from the beginning strained human credibility, and it strains human credibility still. It begins to be credible when we reflect, first, that there is the antecedent affinity between God and man as made in the divine image, with the potentiality of the greatest fellowship between creator and creature that is imaginable; and second, that the essence of deity is self-giving love, with a potentiality of self-giving beyond the measure of human analogies. It is this which St John goes on to mention when he adds the words 'We saw his glory'. The glory of Jesus is the glory of self-giving love shown in splendour in his life and finally in his death.

Such were the ways in which the Christians of the apostolic age came to think of the relation between Jesus and God.[5] The experience of the followers of Jesus led them to an attitude of worship towards him and to a recognition that his sovereignty was a sovereignty not only over themselves but in relation to the world. Their belief gave to Jesus a supra-historical status, and this was expressed in the imagery of coming down from heaven, or being sent into the world, or of emptying himself to become Man (Phil. 2.6–7), or being rich and becoming poor (II Cor. 8.9). No doubt thoughts of a local heaven in the skies above our local earth were in mind, but it was realized that the reality that was believed was not a matter of localities. No one supposed or supposes that deity travelled through space to visit this planet at Bethlehem. Deity is everywhere, beyond and within, within and beyond; and the risen Jesus shares in this omnipresence. The imagery of beyondness tells of the contrast of creator and creature, God and man; and the beyondness of the divine Jesus denotes him as one who is more than the product of history, for in him God uniquely acted in history. But Jesus is within as well as beyond; and the Johannine prologue, while affirming the beyondness of Jesus in the imagery of 'coming', tells also of the claim that Jesus is the climax of the process of the divine Word who

[5] John Knox, op. cit., p. 54, distinguishes helpfully between 'event Christologies' and 'form Christologies'. The former ask what God was doing through Jesus; the latter ask what Jesus is himself by definition.

had always been at work within nature and history as life and light.

In surveying the phases in the development of 'Christology', the belief of the Christians of the first era about Jesus Christ, we notice that while the process may begin with questions about titular definitions ('Is Jesus this, or is Jesus that?'), it becomes increasingly apparent how inadequate titular definitions are to express the reality of God in Jesus. This fact has been put very strongly by C. K. Barrett:

He himself had sought no labels, no categories by which to express his lordship within and over the human race. Secure in his knowledge of, trust in and obedience to the Father, he had pursued his way with the authority God had given him, so that those who knew him best, even before the resurrection sealed and universalized the matter, had recognized him as Lord.

And he goes on to say that by its tendency to give Jesus definitive titles the Church was fitting him into 'the niches of accepted greatness' in a way that was contrary to Jesus's own practice.[6] I cannot follow Barrett the whole way in this. Though the titles were and are inadequate, if there is to be thought and communication of truth about Jesus at all there must needs be inspired language for the purpose, while we recognize the inadequacy of language for the reality which Jesus is.

We notice also in the story of early Christology that the belief goes hand in hand with an experience of practical obedience to Jesus's lordship, and in that ex-

[6] C. K. Barrett, *Jesus and the Gospel Tradition*, p. 33.

D

perience the Cross has a very significant place. First the key concept is the Kingdom of God, the living of human lives under God's sovereignty. Then it is seen that the key to the coming of the kingdom was the death and the resurrection of Jesus; and both for the disciples in their approach to the Passion and for the Church in its subsequent life of 'living through dying', to share in the Cross and the risen life is the heart of Christianity. At a later stage St John expounds both the essence of the kingdom and the dying and rising with Jesus under the new category of *glory*. The glory is seen supremely in the Passion, and the disciples and all subsequent believers are to share in it: 'The glory which thou hast given to me, I have given to them' (St John 17.22).[7] In these ways the lordship of Jesus was realized.

III

THE IMPORTANCE, however, of the confession 'Jesus is Lord' is not only that Jesus is divine but that God is Christlike. 'God is Christlike and in him is no un-Christlikeness at all.'

In realizing the meaning of Christ the Church found itself thinking about God in new ways. The doctrine of the Trinity did not arise from speculation or theorizing but from the experience of the first Christians. As they

[7] For the theme of glory as summarizing the New Testament revelation cf. my *The Glory of God and the Transfiguration of Christ*, London: Longmans, 1949; Darton, Longman and Todd, 1968, ch. VIII.

reflected upon their old faith in the God of the Hebrew scriptures together with their recognition of deity in Jesus and of the power within them of the Holy Spirit, they believed themselves to be encountering not a mere set of passing phases in the life of God (the view which appeared in later history under the name of Sabellianism) but deity as he is eternally. Here the teaching of the Fourth Gospel about the love and glory of God is significant, for in the discourse and prayer of Jesus at the supper the love and mutual glorifying of the Father and the Son in the Passion is presented as the disclosure in history of God as he eternally is. The doctrine of the Trinity is the affirmation that self-giving is characteristic of Being, that mutuality of self-giving love belongs to God's perfection; and the self-giving of God towards his creatures is possible because of the glory which the Father has with the Son in the love of the Spirit eternally.[8]

The Christlikeness of God means that his passion and resurrection are the key to the very meaning of God's own deity. Is there within and beyond the universe any coherence or meaning or pattern or sovereignty? The

---

[8] Cf. A. A. Vogel, *The Next Christian Epoch*, p. 89: 'The doctrine of the Trinity is more basic than the doctrine of God's Fatherhood of the world, for the Trinity indicates how God can be our Father. God is able to create things outside himself and be their Father because he lives a life of eternal "begetting" and "bestowing" within himself. His activity in creating and giving himself to a world that differs from him mirrors the fecundity of his Being within himself; his being in Word, Love, Dialogue, Life.' Cf. the same author's *The Christian Person*, New York: Seabury Press, 1968, pp. 98–106.

New Testament doctrine is that in the death and resurrection of Jesus, in the fact of living through dying, of
finding life through losing it, of the saving of self through
the giving of self, there is this sovereignty. And to believe
it with more than a bare intellectual consent is to believe
it existentially, and to believe it existentially is to follow the way of finding life through losing it. Those who
make their own the living-through-dying of Jesus find
purpose, sovereignty, deity, in and beyond the world.

So when God became incarnate as man his meaningfulness as God came into its own. The self-giving, the
becoming-man, the suffering love were not additions
to the divine experience or mere incidents in the divine
history. In becoming man, God revealed the meaning of
what it is to be God. But he could do so not because he
is incomplete without man or dependent upon creatures
for his own existence, but because he is in himself the
perfection of love. The glory is seen in the becoming-
man because it is a glory 'beyond' and eternal.

So, too, in Jesus the human race finds its own true
meaning. Men rejected Jesus because they preferred the
glory of man to the glory of God, as St John draws
out in his gospel. But the glory which they preferred, and
still prefer in their folly, is not man's true glory but the
false glory of self-centredness, self-assertion and pride.
Man's true glory is the reflection in him of the divine
glory, the self-giving love seen in Jesus.

Thus it is in Jesus that we see man becoming his true
self, in that giving away of self which happens when man
is possessed by God. The meaning of what it is to be

man appears when man is the place where deity fulfils himself, and the glory of the one is the glory of the other. The phrase 'the Man for others' is an illuminating one, but it is not the whole story, for God created man not only for others but for God.

SIX

From Faith to Faith

I

AMIDST the conflicts of theology which we have been considering in the previous chapters of this book the Christian belief in the Triune God stands, both illuminating the conflicts and illuminated by them.

If secular Christianity is in danger of losing Christian identity it is none the less within the secular city and not apart from it that the meaning of transcendence must be rediscovered. If Christian atheism is an incredible mythology the answer to it is a costly rediscovery of the Christlikeness of deity. If the idea that the universe has a centre and a moral shape is no longer accepted as axiomatic in religious and ethical discussion, the answer is for Christians not to cling to facile assumptions but to learn again that it is only in the light of the Cross that all things work together for good. If an existentialist version of Christianity does far less than justice to what Christianity means it may yet be along an existentialist path that the fuller reality can be found and reaffirmed. If technology gives no answer to man's deepest predicaments the answer will be given by Christians who know that the divine Spirit is within the technological city. So, too, the inadequacy of the world's religions will be shown only by Christians who reverence in them the divine logos who lightens every man.

In all these ways the authority of Christian theology
to correct and expose misleading trends of thought is
linked with the humility which learns from the contemporary world and is awake to the divine energies within
it. The Incarnation was not only the condescension of
Creator to creature, of infinite to finite, but also the
condescension of the wisdom of the divine Word to the
modes of human utterance. Jesus, the Word, spoke the
Aramaic of his time and expressed the meaning of the
divine kingdom partly through the imagery of Hebrew
prophecy and apocalyptic and partly through parables
drawn from the everyday life of his hearers. The Church
in its proclamation of Jesus as the Wisdom and the
Word is called to follow the way of the Incarnation.
It has used languages, images, analogies and philosophies. The belief of the Church that the formulation of
its doctrine has been by divine inspiration does not alter
its recognition that all language is inadequate to the
mystery of God in Christ. The task of interpreting its
faith in a particular age and culture is beset by danger
on either side. There is the danger of theology becoming
assimilated to the world's wisdom in a false secularity,
and there is the danger of theology becoming meaningless through not learning from the world which it sets
out to teach. If theology would avoid the dangers of a
false secularization the sure safeguard is to keep at its
heart the essential Christian attitudes of creature to
Creator, of sinner to Saviour. It is when we have lost
the attitude of the worshipper, of awe and reverence in
the presence of the Other, and when we have ceased to

ask forgiveness for our sins, that the line has been crossed. It is on this line that the crisis for secular Christianity is located.

It is the role of the contemporary conflicts of theology to expose the *idolatries* to which we Christians are prone; and the exorcism of them is necessary for the renewal of faith and for the convincing communication of faith to the world. Idolatry for Christians wears many guises. It arises when the service of God becomes so 'religionized' that men become blind to the challenges of God in everyday episodes; but it can arise also when the service of God becomes so activist that there is no room for the contemplation of God as the author and the goal of human service. It arises perhaps most frequently when the concepts and images of God, and our own way of realizing them, become 'absolutized' and so replace the reality whom they represent. In all these ways we can 'turn our glory into the likeness of a calf that eats hay'.

The remedy for idolatry is the recovery of all the aspects of Faith as the New Testament writers present it. Faith includes assent to the pattern of things believed. It includes the recognition that God is. It includes personal self-committal to Christ as the Lord. It includes the staking all upon an overwhelming probability to be tested by acceptance in action. It includes trust in God to act powerfully beyond our asking. It includes the attitude of one who sets out on a journey not knowing what the end will be. And it includes the trustful perseverance through the blackness of doubt, uncertainty, despair. Faith is not security away from darkness, it is the will to go on with darkness all around.

II

IF THE conflicts which we have been discussing can serve what one of the Collects in the Book of Common Prayer calls 'the more confirmation of the faith' it will be through a deeper and more dynamic understanding of the authority and message of the Bible. The true radicalism in theology does not try to find substitutes for the Bible but to explore the roots of its authority.

The Bible is not infallible. It could not be precisely so, as there is uncertainty as to the exact Hebrew and Greek text which the authors write; and there are plenty of contradictions in historical passages within it. It contains many literary media besides literal history. Again, the Bible is not itself revelation, for revelation is the delivery by God of his truth through the words of the Bible to men in their particular contexts in history; and revelation is that total process, including the words of scripture, the Holy Spirit and the Christian community:

For scripture is not a frozen or petrified record, but something which comes alive only in the ongoing life of the community which first gave birth to scripture and has since proclaimed and interpreted the teaching of scripture.[1]

[1] John Macquarrie, *Principles of Christian Theology*, p. 10.

The revelation which is made known through the Bible acts not in a vacuum but in the context of what is historically known as Tradition and Reason. Tradition does not mean that the Church has teachings which supplement those of the Bible or constitute an additional corpus of revelation. It means rather that it is within the common life, the worship and the general mind of the Christian community that the Christian is attuned to the understanding of the biblical message. The appeal to Reason means that all genuine sciences in the world can assist in the understanding of the Bible, and the history of the last century has shown how this can happen. Such is the mode of the authority of the Bible in the service of divine revelation.

Now in modern times attempts have been made to recover the authority of the Bible in ways which are *prima facie* impressive but stultify their own purpose. There has been the appeal to the Bible in a literalistic or infallibilistic way, and this can both freeze the dynamism of the Bible's own message and make the claim of the Bible unacceptable to the scientifically minded. There has also been 'Biblical theology' which, using critical methods, interprets the Bible in its main theological themes but concentrates on understanding the Bible 'from within' and eschews the use of non-biblical categories for the understanding of the message. So, too, the return to Tradition for the understanding of the Bible has sometimes meant recovering the correct formulations of the historic faith in a way that can miss the dynamism of the biblical word. So, too, the upholding of Reason as the clue can sometimes mean the picking from the Bible of those elements which are congruous with some limited modern rationalism.

The recovery of the authority of the Bible calls for the revival in depth of every one of the aspects of the process of revelation and the bringing of the process into relation with the modern world.

Thus the Bible's own categories need to be allowed to come alive by being taken seriously – Fatherhood, holiness, mercy, judgement – and we will know and declare that our God is not a pet-name for human activities but is One who raises the dead. But the realization of this will come through the finding of the God of the Bible in the concrete human situations of today, and it will be tested through our power to use interpretative analogies in the Bible's own manner of parable.

Tradition will be our guide to the interpretation of the Bible through the appeal to the total life and experience of the Church from the ancient Fathers (with their important role) onwards. But Tradition will be recovered not as a petrified catena of doctrinal norms, but as the lively activity of the Christian community, its members serving one another and serving the world and so being the corporate scene in which the message of the Bible is dynamically felt and understood. The common life of the Church will interpret the Bible not as the protector of its contents so much as the divine-human encounter in which the Word of God is heard.

So, too, will Reason aid the understanding of the

Bible, not only through the bringing of scholarly studies
to bear upon its history, its language and its text but
through all those studies of the *world* as the scene of the
activity of the divine Word so that the knowledge of
what he is doing in the world will illuminate and be
illuminated by the message of the Word of salvation.
It is through this work of interpretation that the Bible's
own history and categories become not less but more
authoritative as declaring the meaning of God and the
meaning of man.

It was said earlier in this book that there are three
broad types of philosophy which theology today finds
at hand to try to use: existentialism, empiricism and
process philosophy. It is time to mention the third,
for it bears upon the biblical theme of the divine
Word in nature and history.

The most arresting treatment of a Christian view of
the world along lines of process philosophy in recent
times, and perhaps in any times, is found in the writings
of Teilhard de Chardin. In one sense his thesis may seem
not to be new. It is in line with a series of theologians,
not least in England, who have found deity manifesting
himself in developing degrees of significance through the
evolution of nature with man as the climax. In outline
this was the theme of Charles Gore's Bampton lectures,
The Incarnation of the Son of God (1891) and of William Temple's *Christus Veritas* (1925). In greater fulness it was the theme of Lloyd Morgan's Gifford lectures *Life, Mind and Spirit*, and of Lionel Thornton,

C.R.'s *The Incarnate Lord* (1928) which made use of
A. N. Whitehead's philosophy of organism for a Christian understanding of the universe. C. E. Raven treated
the theme somewhat in the manner of Lloyd Morgan
in his Gifford lectures of 1951–52 on *Natural Religion
and Christian Theology*, and Raven's theme, here as
elsewhere, is marked by his emphasis upon the Cross as
the key to a principle of living-through-dying which is
the secret of man's place in the universe.

These older writings meant little or nothing to the
Barthian theologians on the Continent and in America.
But to those schooled in them Teilhard's thesis did
not come as wholly new. However, what is new in him
is not just that he sees divine significance in the
general phenomenon of emergent evolution, but that he
is able to argue from his own scientific investigations
into the processes of nature that there is a 'Christliness'
at a number of points in the process, which postulates a
'divine-ness' belonging to the whole and to its beginning and its goal. How far his thesis is at once scientifically and philosophically watertight it has been found
hard both by scientists and by philosophers to say, and a
theologian may feel modestly unsure whether Teilhard's argument as he develops it leads to transcendent
deity or deity virtually within and identical with the
natural processes.[2] But uncertainty as to whether the
former interpretation holds good in respect of Teil-

[2] Macquarrie confesses to uncertainty on this in his illuminating
analysis of Teilhard's thesis, cf. *Studies in Christian Existentialism*, ch. 13. It has also to be considered what place sin and
redemption have in Teilhard's thesis.

hard's argument does not alter Teilhard's passionate conviction about deity in relation to the world. And many men and women, unconcerned about the coherence of his theory, have learned from his books a new spirituality, a spirituality which looks at the world as the sciences know it and sees in it everywhere the awe and wonder of the divine presence. The success or failure of Teilhard's philosophy does not alter his power to stir imaginations to a new sensitivity to the world as God's world.

Teilhard's work seems prophetic of the birth of a new religious imagery. In *The Future of Man* he wrote:

In the narrow, partitioned and static Cosmos wherein our fathers believed themselves to dwell, Christ was 'lived' and loved by His followers, as He is today, as the Being on whom all things depend, in whom the Universe finds its 'substance'. But this Christological function was not easily defended on rational grounds, at least if the attempt was made to interpret it in a full, organic sense. Accordingly Christian thinking did not specially seek to incorporate it in any precise Cosmic order. At that time the Royalty of Christ could be readily expressed in terms of His ascendancy through moral law. . . . But in a universe of 'Conical' structure Christ has a place (the apex!) ready for Him to fill, whence His Spirit can radiate through all the centuries and all beings; and because of the genetic links running through all the levels of Time and Space between the elements of a convergent world, the Christ-influence, far from being restricted to the mysterious 'zones' of Grace, spreads and penetrates throughout the entire mass of Nature in movement. In such a world Christ cannot sanctify the Spirit without (as the Greek Fathers intuitively perceived) uplifting and saving the totality of Matter. Christ becomes truly universal to the full extent of our Christian needs.[3]

If there are even fragments of truth in Teilhard's understanding of the world, then the older imagery, such as the divine spirit brooding over the waters of chaos, may give place to imagery derived from the world of the sciences. It is thus that Teilhard may be a prophet for the bewildering age which lies before us, as St Augustine was a prophet for the bewildering age which followed the sack of the city of Rome.[4] But where St Augustine was Latin, Teilhard was recapturing the spirit of the Greek Fathers; and while St Augustine was prophetic of the reconstruction of the civilization of the West, Teilhard's concern was with the re-creation of the world through Christ.

III

THEOLOGY NEEDS openness. So often a lack of openness has vitiated theology in its tasks. Through lack of openness to the contemporary world theology has sometimes worked in a kind of vacuum with neither meaningfulness for itself nor power of self-communication. But through lack of openness to the past theology can be so obsessed with the contemporary as to lose a true perspective and give to the contemporary far less than it can. And openness to the world must

[3] Teilhard de Chardin, *The Future of Man*, London: Collins; New York: Harper and Row, 1964, p. 94.

[4] I owe this parallel to Thomas Corbishley, S.J., *Contemporary Christians*, ch. 6.

always be accompanied by an openness to Christ crucified, or else the world's wisdom can mislead. The need is for every kind of openness – to the past and to the present, to the world and to heaven and eternity.

By openness to the *past* the Christian can contemplate the life and death and Resurrection of Jesus. It is humbling to be made to realize that the world before or since has produced nothing so worthy of contemplation because what is there given is from beyond the world. The life of Jesus is to be imitated, and the death and Resurrection of Jesus are to be shared. So the sacraments of the Church which convey the death and the Resurrection to the believers link the contemplation of the past with the reality of the present. There must no less be openness to the past in the many centuries between the historic Christ and today. The saintly lives of the past encourage us, and we discover that new truths or errors are often in fact the re-emergence of old ones.

But the deepest significance of the past is that it contains reflections of what is *eternal*. Saintly men and women of any age belong to more than their own era; they 'transcend'. Therefore openness to heaven is necessary for a Christian. Heaven is the final meaning of man as created in God's own image for lasting fellowship with God. Openness to heaven is realized in the Communion of Saints in deliberate acts of prayer and worship. But it is realized no less in every act of selflessness or humility or compassion, for such acts are already anticipations of heaven in the here and now.

Thus our openness to heaven is null and void unless it carries with it an openness to the world around us. Within the daily decisions and relationships of the world around us we encounter God, and we learn the meaning of our theology in human terms. Those who would isolate the secular city from the past and from eternity lose the dimension in which human lives have their ultimate meaning and the perspective in which the needs of the secular city are rightly seen. But equally those who would aspire devoutly to heaven without realizing the anticipations of heaven to be found within the secular city are aiding the false dichotomy which is the cause of many evils.

Nowhere more vividly than in the sacrament of the Eucharist do Christians find through Christ an openness to the past and to the present, to heaven and to the world. The sacrifice of Christ on Calvary is present in the here and now in its timeless potency, and the homely bread and wine of a contemporary meal are made the effectual signs of Christ's self-giving. The Christian community on earth is one with the saints in heaven. Blending past and present, earth and heaven, the Eucharist is a prophecy and a prayer for our coming to the vision of God and for the coming of God's reign in the world.

Through this openness the Christian is equipped to tackle the tasks of the present with realism and to face the future with hope. The Christian hope is always twofold, for the vision of God and for the coming of the reign of God in the world. But, immediately, the call to a Christian is to share in the death and resurrection of Jesus Christ, in the way of living through dying, of losing life so as to find it. Such is the life with Christ and in Christ, who is at once the Man for others and true God.

Bibliography

ALTIZER, T. J. J., *The Gospel of Christian Atheism*, Philadelphia: The Westminster Press, 1966; London: Collins, 1967.

BARRETT, C. K., *Jesus and the Gospel Tradition*, London: S.P.C.K., Philadelphia: Fortress Press, 1968.

BARTSCH, H. W. (ed.), *Kerygma and Myth*, London: S.P.C.K., 1953.

BORNKAMM, G., *Jesus of Nazareth*, London: Hodder & Stoughton; New York: Harper and Row, 1960.

BULTMANN, R., *Jesus and the Word*, London: Fontana Books, 1958; New York: Scribners
Theology of the New Testament, Vols. One and Two, New York: Scribners; London: SCM Press, 1952–55.

BUREN, PAUL VAN, *The Secular Meaning of the Gospel*, New York: Macmillan; London, SCM Press, 1963.

BURKITT, F. C., *The Gospel History and its Transmission*, Edinburgh: T. & T. Clark, 1906.

CHARDIN, TEILHARD DE, *The Future of Man*, London: Collins; New York: Harper and Row, 1964.

CORBISHLEY, T., *Contemporary Christians*, London: Geoffrey Chapman, 1966.

COX, HARVEY: *The Secular City*, New York: Macmillan; London, SCM Press, 1965.

DODD, C. H., *History and the Gospel*, London: Hodder Paperbacks, 1964.

EASTON, B. S., *The Gospel before the Gospels*, New York: Scribners, 1929.

FULLER, R. H., *The Foundations of New Testament Christology*, London: Lutterworth Press; New York: Scribners, 1965.
The Mission and Achievement of Jesus, London: SCM Press, 1954.

GORE, CHARLES, *The Incarnation of the Son of God*, 1891.

Historicity and Chronology in the New Testament, London: S.P.C.K., 1965.

HOOKER, M. D., *The Son of Man in Mark*, London: S.P.C.K., 1967.

HOSKYNS, E. C. and DAVEY, F. N., *The Riddle of the New Testament*, London: Faber, 1931.

JAMES, ERIC (ed.), *Spirituality for Today*, London: SCM Press, 1968.

JENKINS, DAVID, *The Glory of Man*, London: SCM Press; New York: Scribners, 1967.

KNOX, JOHN, *The Humanity and Divinity of Christ*, Cambridge University Press, 1967.

MACQUARRIE, J., *God and Secularity*, Philadelphia: Westminster Press; London: Lutterworth Press, 1968.

Principles of Christian Theology, New York: Scribners, 1966; London: SCM Press, 1967.

Studies in Christian Existentialism, London: SCM Press, 1965; Philadelphia: Westminster Press, 1966.

MANSON, T. W., *The Background of the New Testament and its Eschatology*, Cambridge University Press, 1956.

MORGAN, LLOYD, *Life, Mind and Spirit*, London: Williams & Norgate.

NINEHAM, D. E., *Commentary on St Mark*, London: Penguins, 1963.

OGDEN, S. M., *The Reality of God*, New York: Harper & Row, 1966; London: SCM Press, 1967.

PITTENGER, N. (ed.), *Christ for Us Today*, London: SCM Press, 1968.

RAMSEY, A. M., *The Glory of God and the Transfiguration of Christ*, London: Longmans, 1949; Darton, Longman and Todd, 1968.

From Gore to Temple, London: Longmans, 1960.

Sacred and Secular, London: Longmans; New York: Harper and Row, 1965.

RAMSEY, I. T., *Religious Language*, London: SCM Press; New York: Macmillan, 1957.

RAVEN, C. E., *Natural Religion and Christian Theology*, Cambridge University Press, 1953.

ROBINSON, J. A. T., *Honest to God*, London: SCM Press; Philadelphia: Westminster Press, 1963.

SCHWEITZER, ALBERT, *The Quest of the Historical Jesus*, London: A. & C. Black, 3rd ed., 1953; New York: Macmillan

SELWYN, E. G. (ed.), *Essays Catholic and Critical*, London: S.P.C.K., 1926.

TEMPLE, WILLIAM, *Christus Veritas*, 1925.

THORNTON, LIONEL, *The Incarnate Lord*, London: Longmans, 1928.

VOGEL, A. A., *The Next Christian Epoch*, New York: Harper & Row, 1966.

The Christian Person, New York: Seabury Press, 1968.

Index of Names and Subjects

INDEX   125

Ramsey, I. T., 50
Rationalism, 110
Raven, C. E., 112
Reason, 109, 110
Religion, 17
Resurrection, the, 52, 53, 77,
    78, 79, 80, 89, 91, 93, 115
Revelation, 108ff.
Righteousness, 84, 85
Robinson, J. A. T., 9, 87

Sacraments, the, 44
Schmidt, K. L., 70
Schweitzer, Albert, 67f.
Secular, the, 15
Secular City, The, 7, ch. 1
    passim, 116
Secularism, 7, 9, 16, 17, 18, 19,
    37
  and Christianity, 18f.
Sex, 27
Sociology, 23
Son of Man, 88, 90
Suffering, 41
Supernatural, the, 26
Symbol, 60f., 73f.

Technology, 15, 19ff., 27
Teilhard de Chardin, 50, 111,
    112, 113f.
Temple, William, 33, 40, 111
Theism, 9, 22, 24, 26, 33, 34,
    35, 37, 38, 39, 43, 59, 60
Theology, 16, 18f., 39, 40, 53,
    54, 77, 105, 106, 107, 116
  biblical, 18, 19, 43, 109
  existential, 47, 49, 51, 56,
    105
  philosophical, 59
Thornton, Lionel, 111f.
Tradition, 109, 110
Transcendence, 7, 23, 26, 27,
    28, 29, 37
Trinity, doctrine of the, 40, 60,
    98, 99
Tyrrell, G., 67

Violence, 27
Vogel, Arthur, 10, 28f., 36, 99

Whitehead, A. N., 50, 112
Worship, 25, 56f., 91, 115

Index of Biblical References